SEX IN MAN AND WOMAN

SEX
IN MAN AND WOMAN

Its Emotional Variations

by

THEODOR REIK

VISION

Vision Press Limited
11–14 Stanhope Mews West
London SW7 5RD

ISBN 0 85478 313 X

First published in the British Commonwealth 1975

Printed in Great Britain by
Clarke, Doble & Brendon Ltd., Plymouth
MCMLXXV

Contents

Introduction

This contribution to the comparative psychology of the sexes, especially of their emotional divergencies, continues and complements an essay which I wrote four years ago, published under the title of "The Emotional Differences of the Sexes."* If that essay was the harvest of many seasons, the following paragraphs present the gleanings.

The grandmothers of this generation did not approve of sexuality. Modern Americans acknowledge its importance, but one must be courageous not to try to minimize the emotional differences of the sexes. The horrifying and all pervasive tendency toward equalization—a kind of mania which governs our mentality—seems to result in these deep-rooted differences being brushed aside and almost contemptuously dismissed.

The divergencies of course originate in biological distinctions, but they are not restricted to them. It is more than seventy-five years ago since two British biologists, Patrick Geddes and I. Arthur Thomson, published their book *The Evolution of Sexes*. In tracing the properties of the two sexes to the animals, they demonstrated how the two sexes are complementary and mutually dependent, and said: "While

* Contained in *Of Love and Lust*, New York, 1957.

there are broad general distinctions between the intellectual and especially the emotional characteristics of males and females among the higher animals, these not infrequently tend to become mingled. There is, however, no evidence that they might be gradually obliterated."

In the seventy-five years since that book was published, great changes in the social and psychological position of the sexes have taken place. Women have achieved the right to vote and their place in society has changed. Yet the telling sentence written then has still remained valid: "What was decided among the Prehistoric Protozoa cannot be annulled by an act of Parliament." While we give lip service to the theory of the divergent psychology of the sexes, we treat men and women in our thoughts as though they were one sex. Yet the sober and unbiased view of the emotional and mental life of the sexes offers contrary, conflicting and complementary pictures. Husband and wife have a common life, but not an identical one. Life would be intolerable if it were otherwise: if men were to think and act like women, and women like men. How would you like an opera in which only female or only male singers were heard? Wouldn't it be likely to be boring and monotonous? Even slogans such as "liberty" and "the pursuit of happiness" mean different things for women and for men. Even the Ten Commandments are not conceived as equally binding on both of them. There are moments—and not only moments—in which those basic distinctions are revealed as in a flash. A man or a woman becomes then suddenly aware that he or she is worlds distant not only from the individual person of the other sex, but from the whole of the other sex. It is as if it became obvious in a split minute that men and women live on different planets, move in different orbits.

Properly seen this book is not a scientific work. It deals with the psychology of the average man and woman, but there are no such animals. It presents the differences between the sexes without again and again adding that there is something of the most feminine in the most masculine man and something of the most masculine in the most feminine woman. I hope that the reader will take this constantly for granted.

The loose arrangement and the informal tone of these contributions are to be explained by the manner in which they came into existence. They were jotted down, mostly in the evening hours—after I had had many psychoanalytical sessions with patients or after students had discussed their psychoanalytic cases with me. In this sense, the observations presented here resemble by-products of psychoanalytic practice, similar to the material that every large industry produces. Such by-products need not always be used immediately, but should not be discarded because the day may come when they will be useful. These psychological observations and tentative conclusions are born, so to speak, on the wrong side of the scientific track. This does not exclude the fact that they may not one day acquire respectability.

A benevolent critic, John Dollard, professor of Psychology at Yale, considered the results of my research in "Emotional Differences of the Sexes" "seminal propositions." Also this section is, to quote him, "not science, though it is the kind of thing of which science will one day be made."

Overture in ¾ Time

When Fred Goodman and I took an afternoon walk together one day in Central Park, it was late in November, but

the weather was summer-like. We had not seen each other
since I had returned from Europe.

Fred is the only friend I have kept from childhood on.
Our parents knew each other and for some years we lived
in the same house. His family was financially better off than
mine, but we were born and reared in the same middle-
class Viennese-Jewish milieu. He is exactly four weeks older
than I am—we have passed seventy-two—but he likes to act
the older, sadder and wiser man. With his thick white
hair and clean-shaven face he makes a much more youthful
impression than I who am an old, bald codger. Fred likes
to argue and does this especially vehemently when he really
agrees with me.

He had recognized the signals of approaching National
Socialism in Vienna earlier and much more clearly than I
and had already escaped Hitler in 1933. He had then lived
in Paris for a few years. Of his family only his younger sister,
Anna, and her two children had perished in the gas cham-
bers of Auschwitz.

Even before he came to America some of his novels had
become best sellers. He always had more success than I. Yet,
in spite of all this, he was not happy.

When we were in high school we had certain common
daydreams which we sometimes discussed. I remember that
we were still talking them over a few days before we grad-
uated. We both wanted to become famous, to make our
names known far beyond the frontiers of our Austria—yes,
even beyond Europe. Even when he was in high school, Fred
had spoken of becoming a novelist while I had finally decided
to study psychology. He saw his wish fulfilled when he became a well-known writer in his late twenties, while my

first psychoanalytical books awakened only the interest of a very narrow circle of readers. He is, it seems, satisfied with his *métier* as he calls it, while I sometimes think that being a psychoanalyst is less a profession than a calamity.

In contrast to his usual talkativeness, Fred was monosyllabic during our walk that afternoon. He seemed absorbed. Finally he said, "You know, something strange happened to me when I came here on the bus. There was a very pretty young woman sitting across from me. I felt she was looking at me all the time. Suddenly, when I got out, she was beside me, speaking. . . ."

"Well," I said, "nothing remarkable to that. It happens to many men in New York."

"*Tais-toi, mon vieux!*" Fred said in his lofty manner. He occasionally uses French phrases in our conversation, which is usually held in our Viennese-German. "You have rotten manners, Theodor. You never let a man finish what he is going to say. Now that lovely lady asked: 'Aren't you Fred Goodman? I thought I recognized you from the photographs on the jackets of your books. I am an enthusiastic reader of yours and have often wanted to write you a fan letter.' "

"Still nothing remarkable," I said. "Everybody knows how vain writers are—the present one not excluded—"

"Let me finish. There was certainly nothing remarkable in that, and such things have happened to me several times before; but right then I was preoccupied with my new novel. The chatting of the young, pretty woman only disturbed me. It was a nuisance and I wished she would leave me alone. When at last she did, I remembered how often I had roamed through the streets of Vienna as a boy. I was shy and lonely and I often daydreamed that just such a young girl might come up to me, that she would address me and we would begin to talk. She would understand what a really special guy I was. . . . Soon she would fall in love with me and—"

"It would end in a small hotel auf der Wieden,"* I interrupted.

"Perhaps. But when that charming young woman left me a while ago, I suddenly found myself thinking of that miracle which never happened in my youth. You know I don't share your shallow and rationalistic atheism. I believe in a god or, if you like, an omnipotent demi-urge who fulfills our wishes. But he always fulfills them too late when we cannot enjoy their realization any longer. The sad part of it is that, however late, we still remember how wonderful it would have been had they been fulfilled twenty, or even ten, years earlier. I believe Yahweh became anti-Semitic, like so many other Israelites. At best, He has become tolerant since He has 'arrived.' When He now remembers His past, He perhaps casually remarks: 'Some of my best friends were Jews.' He is, I believe, this master of irony who fulfills our wishes after we don't feel them any longer."

"Fred, what's the matter with you? Why so bitter?"

"I will go further and perhaps you will understand. Remember the Third Caffeehaus in the Prater?"

"Of course I do." There were three larger outdoor cafés in the big Viennese park called the Prater. Families liked to visit them especially during the summer months on Sunday afternoons. Military bands played the merry and sentimental tunes of the contemporary Viennese composers. We sat at simple tables under the chestnut trees until evening. Fred's

* Suburb of Vienna. Allusion to an old song by Leopoldi, "*Ich kenn' auf der Wieden ein kleines Hotel.*"

parents had sometimes taken me there together with him
and his sister Anna when I was a boy.

"Do you remember the 'Salamuci'?"

Of course I remembered. There was always an Italian
fellow there who went from table to table selling various
delicacies. He had a scale and a knife with him and sliced
hard Italian salami and Emmenthaler cheese which was
served to the guests on paper napkins. All Viennese called
the man "Salamucci."

"How we kids loved that salami!" Fred continued. "As
soon as he arrived Anna and I followed Salamucci with our
eyes and avidly waited until he came over to us. Our father
sometimes bought us salami and cheese. I still remember the
pleading glance mother would give him when the Salamucci
approached our table. You just can't imagine how much I
wanted that salami! I decided then and there as a little boy
that some day when I was grown up I would buy a whole
salami and eat it all by myself. As a student I couldn't, of
course, afford to buy a whole wurst, and later I forgot. . . .
A few months ago, I happened to cross the Italian quarter
here—'Little Italy,' you know. I saw there, hanging in the
window of a store, exactly such a whole, hard salami! I rushed
in and bought it and as I carried it home my mouth was
watering. I sliced it exactly as the Salamucci had in the
Prater—big thick slices. You can guess what happened. I
have dental plates! I could not bite through the salami!
I gave it to our colored maid who thoroughly enjoyed it.
When I looked at her and saw the obvious pleasure with
which she ate it in the kitchen, I was so envious I could have
strangled her. That salami became almost a symbol of the
irony of destiny—of the malicious *forza del destino*' that

pervades our life. . . . In my late teens I was tortured by sexual desires. I often could not fall asleep, haunted by fantasies of voluptuous women with whom I had orgies. You know how shy I was with women. A few years ago I met just such a woman as I had imagined as an adolescent boy. I was, of course, no longer shy and she made open advances. As a matter of fact she did her level best. Well, it is certainly not necessary to follow up with the comparison of the salami."

"A few years ago, you say? Didn't Oliver Wendell Holmes, when he was older than you, see a very pretty woman pass by and, sighing, say: 'Oh, to be seventy again.'?"

"The venerable physician was a victim of transparent self-deception. He confused in his memory the intensity of desire with the ability of performance."

"Are you trying to tell me, Fred, that a man in his seventies will not sexually function any longer . . . ?"

Fred dismissed the interruption and continued, "Even if the performance were complete, it is not really the same thing any longer. If the aim is only to prove to oneself or to one's partner that one is still potent, there is little room left for pleasure of the other kind."

"Well," I said, "there remains only resignation which need not be quiet desperation. Socrates in his old age sacrificed a cock to Asclepius in gratitude because he was finally freed from the tyranny of Eros."

"That is very likely since he was married to Xantippe. He must have served Eros with grim determination during his married life. . . . I am tired. Let's go over there to that shady bench and sit down. You did not tell me much about Vienna. Is the old charm still felt there?"

"Yes," I answered. "The music, the women, the atmosphere. People are, if possible, even more courteous than before. Where else in the world would waiters while they serve you wish 'good appetite'? Where else would the loudspeaker at every railway station add to their official announcements, 'We wish you a happy voyage.' It is still wonderful—"

"You are kind enough to overlook how much hypocrisy and insincerity there is in this politeness. The other day I met Carl Finestein—you remember him, don't you?—who had just returned from our beloved city after an absence of twenty-three years. He could have told you plenty about the 'golden Viennese heart.' You know that his whole family was killed in Auschwitz by the Nazis. He ran into an old gentile acquaintance on the street in Vienna. This man had certainly been *Ober-Gauführer* or *Sturmtruppen-Commandant* during that Nazi time, but he greeted Carl most cordially, as though none of this had ever been. When they spoke of the Hitler period, the man said, 'Well, you had it good in America. You had a fine time there and could even earn money while here we had to suffer under Hitler.' The man, no doubt, had been one of the first to shout 'Heil Hitler!' when the Führer entered Vienna."

Just then a group of teen-agers sat down on the bench across from us. We listened to their laughter and observed how the boys teasingly tickled the girls, who pretended to be very annoyed by the attentions of the young men. I pointed to the young people and said: "Just think what a waste of time this whole thing is! Time that could be used for far more valuable things. . . ."

"The question is only whether there really are more valuable things in life."

"Don't forget, Fred, that we are seventy-two!"

"Alas, I can't forget it. Wait—who wrote this?

" 'When our lives become womanless,
Then every light is spent.
For that which then is left to me
I would not give one cent.'*

Oh, yes, that's by Frank Wedekind."

"You will overcome also this crisis of old age," I consoled him. "It will result in resignation and in a short time you will look at it philosophically."

"I feel like Romeo: 'Hang up philosophy! Unless philosophy makes a Juliet.' Don't you feel like that? The only difference is that in our case they had other names: Mitzi and Gretl or Anna."

A girl on the bench across from us shrieked and slapped the boy who had kissed her on the neck. It was then that a tune sounded within me—a familiar waltz tune. What was it? I knew it so well! But the name escaped me. No, it was not a Strauss waltz—neither was it a Lanner or Ziehrer waltz. I must have danced to that tune..... I remembered the Vienna Sophiensäle in which I so often danced as a student. Sometimes we—Fred and I and some friends—went directly from the dance hall to the university because some of our lectures started very early. There were also some polkas and mazurkas, but mostly we danced waltzes. The new dances from America came, of course, much later and were not popular in Vienna at that time. I remember when the old Duchess Pauline Metternich saw the performance of such a new dance for the first time she said, "In my time, they did that in

---

* In the German original:
    Und ist erst das Seelenleben entweibt,
    Dann sind sämtliche Lampen erloschen.
    Für das, was für mich dann noch übrig bleibt,
    Dafür geb' ich nicht einen Groschen.

bed. . . ." Yes those were the days! If I only knew what that tune was that haunted me!

I had been so much absorbed in my quest that I had not heard what Fred had said. "What was that you said about names?" I asked.

"I said that our girls were not called Rosalinde or Juliet, but Mitzi and Gretl and Anna."

Anna! Of course! All of a sudden I knew what the tune was: the waltz from the *Beggar Student* by Millöcker.

> My kiss on her shoulder,
> Was really quite light—
> She, in turn, slapped me
> With all her might.*

The little scene on the bench opposite us, the girl who half-playfully slapped that boy, must have reminded me of the tune. Then Fred had mentioned the name "Anna." But that was the name of his younger sister with whom I was infatuated when I was eighteen years old. The memories of her come back. What did she look like then . . . ? A blond girl with a slightly turned-up nose, and with very nice dimples when she smiled. She often did, too. How happy I was when she laughed at some of my jokes! Yes I wooed her for quite a time. . . . Once when we came back together with some other young people from an excursion in the Viennese woods, I kissed her—and she slapped me! From then on she treated me abominably. It was clear to me that she did not like me and preferred the company of other boys. Oh! There-

---

* In the original:
  Ach ich hab' sie ja nur
  Auf die Schulter geküsst
  Und sie gab mir defür
  Einen Schlag ins Gesicht.

fore the Millöcker tune. I kissed her and she slapped my face! And then came another memory from that time. I had not thought of it for ages. A few weeks after that excursion there was a ball at the Sophiensäle. Yes, I remembered it vividly now. . . . I took a girl friend of Anna's to that dance. I had no money—just the ticket. I couldn't afford to buy her a bouquet of flowers as one did then upon such occasions. A day before the dance, I asked her if she could lend me some money. It would only be for a few days. I even confessed to her that I needed it to get her the flowers. She gave it to me. Therefore the title of the Millöcker operetta: *The Beggar Student*. That is what I was really. I was in my first year at the Vienna University and very poor, earning just enough from tutoring to cover my studies. Fred, too, was at the ball and so was Anna. I did not see much of her. I only greeted her when I passed her on the dance floor.

The next day, when Fred and I discussed the evening and compared notes about the various girls whom we had met, Fred suddenly asked, "By the way, what did you do to my sister last night?" "What did I do?" I asked in astonishment. "I didn't do a thing to her. I just saw her and said 'Hello.' " "I don't believe you," said Fred. "You must have hurt her feelings. When we went home she cried but would not tell me what was the matter. She sobbed later when she was talking to mother at home and I heard your name."

How stupid we were about women when we were young! And, now that we are old, are we much wiser? We know more about them, but do we know them better? There emerged again that waltz tune in me: "My kiss on her shoulder was really quite light. . . ."

Fred broke into my reverie: "I told you about the new

novel I was working on during the summer, didn't I? I am
stuck at the end of only six thousand words."

"What's the plot?" I asked.

"Nothing extraordinary.... The usual—the meeting, mating and misunderstanding of a man and a woman. The plot
is not essential. You seem to think that the string is the most
important part of a necklace. I am searching for a new form
of presentation. Imagine an average young man—let us say
a clerk in a government office—who meets an average young
girl—a secretary or something similar. He feels attracted to
her and she to him."

"I must have read similar things before," I remarked with
too obvious sarcasm.

"No, you haven't. I try to approach the subject in a kind
of alternate *monologue interieur.* You know: first what the
young fellow thinks and feels and then what the girl experiences. Not only towards each other, but towards relatives,
friends, rivals and so on. She and he alone are one thing;
she and he when they are with people are another. I want
to follow not only the development of their relationship, but
their experiences during married life, their tiffs, reconcilia-
tions, escapades, but not in the conventional manner, but
inside out, *Le coeur nue,* so to speak, and not only the heart,
but also what they think in different situations. You get me?"

"Well.... The idea of a double stream of consciousness
had not occurred to me."

"The number of things that don't occur to you is appalling.
The double inner monologue is not the important thing; the
presentation of the secret life of the man and of the woman
is the important thing. The fascinating part of it is the opportunity it gives of changing the viewpoints and of contrasting
what is the 'typically masculine' and the 'typical feminine'

attitude. Not only towards each other, but also to society
and to the world at large. It is as though they lived in two
different worlds. Take, for instance, a scene in a department
store where the man accompanies the girl while she buys a
hat. I would like to give a recording of what he thinks while
she tries on different hats and chats with the salesgirl; then,
again, what she experiences in that situation. Then, I might
perhaps present the girl as she comes to his office in the afternoon to pick him up—how she reacts to that atmosphere."

"A kind of inner duet, so to speak, the soprano and the
tenor alternatively?"

"Yes, but the prose should move as spontaneously, naturally and effortlessly as . . . Mozart's music. Weren't you also
at the Salzburg festival this summer? That little aria 'Give
me your hand, my life' from Don Giovanni sounds as though
Mozart had shaken it out of his sleeve, or rather as if it had
readily fallen from Heaven. Do you know how many versions
there are? How that wonderful genius tried again and again
until he found the exactly appropriate proper? Ah, if one
could achieve something similar to Mozart's music in prose:
the richest content in utmost simplicity. . . ! You are not listening! What are you thinking?"

As a matter of fact I was also thinking of music just then,
but not of immortal Mozart. That waltz tune from *The
Beggar Student* had haunted me again since Fred began talking about the emotional differences between men and women.
Then, as though he had sensed my thoughts, "Didn't you
publish some essays about the emotional divergencies of the
sexes? I remember that paper. There were a few confusions
of the tenses and some other stylistic sloppinesses in it, but
it wasn't bad, not bad at all. That is, for a psychoanalytic
paper. Didn't you plan to continue the series?"

"Well," I said, "I occasionally have flirted with the idea."

"Why don't you marry the idea and make an honest woman of it? Why don't you go ahead and write a little book? I could use some of your insights—with caution, of course. There is, for instance, a scene I have already sketched out for the second part of the novel in which.... What the hell are you laughing about?"

"You know, that really strikes me as funny! It reminds me of the story about the famous violinist who spoke at length about a concert he had given. Finally he said to his friend: "But I am talking all the time about myself! Now tell me about you. What was your impression of my performance of the Beethoven concerto?"

"Well," Fred admitted, a little embarrassed, "I still think you should write that book."

It had begun to rain, one of those fine summer rains, and we walked slowly to the exit of the park. Neither the novel nor the project of my book was mentioned again. We talked of Vienna and of the Salzburg festivals.

I did not give a second thought to our conversation then, but strangely enough I was reminded of it twice during that evening. After dinner I was looking over some magazines I had not seen during the months in Europe. In an issue of *Life* I saw a picture in which an American film star was introduced to the queen in London. On the other side was a man in the same situation before her majesty. The contrast of the curtsey of the woman and the bowing of the man struck me. Turning the pages, I came across the picture of a couple dancing. The arm of the man firmly encircled the waist of the woman, whose arm rested lightly on the man's shoulder. The difference of the man's and the woman's position led my thoughts back to the conversation with Fred that afternoon. Perhaps he is right, I thought. I should look at my notes about the emotional differences of the sexes. There are piles of them in the folders in my drawer over there. But they are disjointed remarks, unconnected observations—sometimes no more than aphorisms.

Nonetheless, tomorrow I'll take a look through at them, examine and shift them, eliminate what is not essential and perhaps add a few new observations. Tomorrow. I am too sleepy now. As I was falling asleep I had a sort of hypnagogic picture. There was that dancing couple from the magazine. For a fleeting moment the young girl became Anna in my imagination and the man myself—as I knew myself from photographs of my student years: a skinny boy with thick, dark hair and eyes full of wonder and longing. And then that waltz tune emerged again, heard with the inner ear, "My kiss on her shoulder was really quite light," and the young couple—Anna and I—danced to it.

PART ONE

Why Can't a Woman Behave Like a Man?

---

1. RESPONSIBILITY FOR THE PRODUCT

The leading character, or rather the not so heroic hero of John P. Marquand's recent novel, *Women and Thomas Harrow*, at a certain point in his ruminations about the emotional differences of the sexes, arrives at a surprising conclusion. This character of Mr. Marquand's is a playwright who has had several successes and also some failures on Broadway. His wife is pregnant for the first time. His thoughts lead him to the point where he compares the opening night of a play with the delivery of the baby. He finds himself complaining that the lot of women is so much easier than that of men! He thinks that a man feels responsible for a play he has written and experiences guilt feelings when the play turns out to be a flop. A woman, he says, does not experience similar feelings when the child she has brought into the world is not perfect.

In many passages of this and other novels, Marquand shows this gift of acute psychological observation. But here he has certainly built up an erroneous theory: a theory which seems strange in a man who is otherwise quite perceptive about women's feelings. The experiences of psychologists as well as gynecologists show just the contrary. They are almost unanimous in the opinion that most women feel responsible for the health and normal condition of their baby. The majority of women feel not only unhappy but clearly guilty if the baby is born with a physical defect or handicap—as though they were responsible for it. Psychoanalysts and gynecologists know the anxieties that many women experience in this regard during their pregnancy. I once observed the case of a very intelligent American woman who was obsessed by the fear that the child with which she was pregnant would be born malformed, or with some serious physical handicap. Driven by this compulsive fear, she went from one gynecologist in Vienna to another, always seeking reassurance in this regard. In her case those fears were determined by concern that the patient might have harmed herself and her genitals when she masturbated as a little girl. Her mother had frequently warned her that she could not have healthy, normal children if she played with herself. The reason for a similar fear in another case was the worry that the baby might have some physical fault due to inherited features. The father of the patient had been, all his adult life, an alcoholic and the mother had had several psychotic breakdowns. Whatever the reasons are in the individual case, it is certainly correct to state that most women feel as responsible for the nature of their baby as the man for the quality of his work.

2. A Surprising Observation

Whoever takes human relations for granted without sometimes wondering about them deprives himself of the great advantage of discovering something original about them— of seeing them in a new light. A chance remark in conversation strikes us occasionally as particularly original or "authentic" although the observed phenomenon had been there before our eyes as well as before those of the next man or woman. We think, for instance, that we know all that is worth knowing about the emotional differences between men and women. Yet some casual sentence of the next man or the next woman hits us by the originality of its observation as though we are seeing these divergencies for the first time. A few remarks made by a patient during a consultation acted as a kind of eye-opener for me the other day. The patient, a man in his late forties, had been divorced twice and was experiencing some difficulties now in his third marriage. His relations with women seemed always to result in a kind of emotional impasse, determined mostly either by his lack of understanding of feminine attitudes or by his impatience with them. Yet his attitude toward "masculine" women was, if possible, still more intolerant than toward very feminine representatives of the opposite sex. Added to other personality difficulties in his profession and his relations with other men, the picture of what we call a "character neurosis" emerged from his description of the situation in which he repeatedly found himself. Considering the disturbance in his relations with women, it was not surprising to hear him complain about his third wife. However, I was baffled by the kind of fault he found in her.

He said, "I cannot stand to be permanently watched." "Watched?" I repeated, astonished. A slight suspicion arose in me. Was this a symptom of a paranoid attitude? It was in the beginning of the psychoanalytic treatment, but until now I had observed nothing that would point in the direction of such a pathological attitude. I had not had the impression that the man was especially mistrustful or vulnerable. There were no delusions or ideas of persecution or grandeur. Neither were there any manifestations of an attitude which makes paranoid patients imagine that all those around them make them the center of their attention—no "ideas of reference," as the psychiatrists call such typical scanning of the environment.

What did he mean? He explained, "You know, women watch you all the time. It is as though you were observed or spied upon as long as you are around them. You get up in the morning and the first glance you feel is that of your wife who wants to discover what mood you are in. You come home from your office and she studies your face as if she wanted to find out whether or not you have had a bad day down town, whether you are cheerful, or tired and fed up. During dinner she looks at you and you feel it is because she wants to know if what she has served you has pleased you. Later, you look up from the paper and you know she has just looked at you wondering if you still love her. Now, don't tell me I imagine all that! Mind you, I do not claim that my wife watches me like a hawk." With a tongue-in-cheek grin he added, "Sometimes I think she watches me as though I were a hawk of which she is afraid. Yet I know she is not afraid of me in the least. She is only eager to find out what I feel—especially about her. You see, it is not important to her to find out what I think of my boss, or of one of my colleagues, or about the government of the United States or American foreign policy. She is not curious about what I feel in regard to God and the world. But she cannot stand the slightest uncertainty about what I think of her. She has to know—or at least to guess— that. Therefore she watches me all the time. I feel as though I were allowed no privacy in my emotional life. No, don't say that I read things into the situation! I happen to know I am right."

He smiled. "I am now so tuned to being watched that I can even conclude from the way she looks at me what she expects me to say about her new dress or hair-do."

His remarks then lost their critical character and became rather humorous. They seemed to make fun of a kind of typical concentration by women on their menfolk. The following thought associations extended his observations beyond the personal to the general: he asserted that the attitude he had observed was characteristic of all women—young and not so young.

For the moment we will put aside several questions which would be of great interest to the psychoanalyst in this context —for instance, the problem of the intense awareness and sensitiveness of the patient. We will also avoid discussing the motives and the origin of the emotional difficulties he always had with women, and neglect the exaggerations in his remarks, which may amount to distortions. It is clear that his sentences are directed by certain tendencies, but we expect this since they occurred during a psychoanalytic session in which uninhibited and unconventional expression of one's feelings are not only permitted, but demanded. We will certainly not consider his generalized observations as the sober, objective opinions of an unbiased observer. There remains the question: is there a grain of truth in them, a core of correct observation that has been neglected or scarcely noticed by the comparative psychology of the sexes?

All generalizations are, we know, unjustified; but there is a grain of truth in the patient's observations—at least as they concern the average woman. This concealed truth becomes manifest when you compare the attitude of the average woman and the average man in everyday married life. It leads us to the conclusion that the woman is not only more attentive to, and more aware of, the mood and its changes than the man—but also more perceptive in regard to it. Her observation is certainly not detached and objective, but personal and extremely keen. Not much escapes her notice. Her watchfulness is selective, yet it is in most cases not restricted to her husband's attitude toward her, although this certainly stands in the foreground of her attention. As a matter of psychological fact many wives wish their husbands would be more aware of their moods and more "attentive" to their feelings.

There are several psychological and sociological reasons for this emotional difference of the sexes, but the fact of an inequal degree of watchfulness is, it seems to me, undeniable. Another question is that of the evaluation of such observations. We will not discuss this question because it is a secondary one here and evaluation is, of course, dependent on the points of view of different persons. Dostoevsky has called psychology a stick with two ends. This is also justified when you have to evaluate a certain attitude of the observed subject. One person might call a man avaricious or stingy while another person might consider the very same man economical or cautious.

As far as I know this divergence of attitude, here sketched, has not been discussed in the scientific literature of comparative psychology. I found a significant contribution to the subject in the play of an author who is certainly acknowledged to have moments of penetrating psychological insights. The first act of Bernard Shaw's *Back to Methusalah* presents scenes between Adam and Eve in the Garden of Eden. They take us back to the beginning of married life. As a matter of fact, Eve is introduced as observer of her mate. She remarks that Adam sits for hours brooding and silent. She has the impression that he hates her in his heart. "When I ask you what I have done to you, you say you are not thinking of me but of the horror of having to be here forever." She thinks he means the horror of having to be here with her forever. Adam sits down sulkily and energetically denies this. He likes her, but does not like himself. The thought that he must endure himself forever is dreadful. He would like to be different, to be better. "Do you never think of that?" he asks. Eve does not: "I am what I am. Nothing can alter that." She does not think about herself, but about him. Now Adam comes to the point: "You are always spying on me. I can never be alone. You always want to know what I have been doing. It is a burden. You should try and have an existence of your own instead of occupying yourself with my existence."

Don't we see here the same impatient feeling toward the woman expressed by my patient during the analytic hour? Don't these sentences of Adam herald a motif whose echo resounded in his descendants? Eve replies what all women would be inclined to say in this situation. She explains the reasons for her watchfulness about which the first husband in the world complained. She has to think of him and watch him because "You are lazy. You are dirty. You neglect yourself. You are always dreaming. You would eat bad food and become disgusting if I did not watch you and occupy myself with you." And some day, in spite of all her care, he might fall on his head and die.

It is not only the first wife and "helpmeet" who speaks thus. It is the mother of all men, the primal mother of all human beings. Her watchfulness toward her mate and her observation of him are the continuation of the attention she has to pay to her children. In Adam—as in all men—lives a boy who would come to harm without such vigilance. The attitude of the first couple in the Garden of Eden repeated itself again and again. It seems that, from the start, Adam was already ungrateful, as we men all are, when we become aware of that particular kind of attention our mothers and wives pay to us. At least no tradition reports that Adam said to his mate after they were expelled from Paradise: "Any old place, just so I am with you."

3. LITTLE GIRLS, LITTLE BOYS

Everything appearing in grown-up men and women was preformed in little boys and girls and the difference in the ways of feelings and thinking of the sexes announces itself early. In the following paragraphs some examples of infantile reactions to everyday life are recorded. In some of them feminine and masculine features are already recognizable in a budding form.

A forty-three-year-old man discusses in his analytic sessions memories of the very early toilet-training to which his mother subjected him. She was proud that the little boy never soiled himself after the second year. The patient reports in connection with this his earliest childhood memory which could be precisely dated and was verified. When the patient was two and a half years old, a sister was born. The little boy was present when the water broke. The father ran out to fetch the physician. The boy contemptuously shouted at mother: "You pig!"

A little boy, growing up at a farm, told a visitor from New York that his parents were roughhousing in the night. In this way the child interpreted the sexual intercourse of his parents. He had often heard the noises from the next bedroom, interpreting them as a fight.

A little girl must also have arrived at a similar concept of the sexual relations of her parents. The patient remembers from her childhood that she thought that her father was mistreating her mother in the night and hurting her. The child conceived of those nightly scenes as continuations of the frequent arguments the parents had during the day. Whenever she could hear the sighs or moans of her mother during the night she was afraid that father was hurting her and she anxiously searched the face of her mother at breakfast for physical traces of the trial of the night.

The father of a boy, not yet two years old, put his watch several times to the ear of his child who enjoyed hearing the tick-tick. Once the boy took the watch and put it to the ear of the father, observing his face. The perceptive father was not satisfied by the explanation that the behavior of his son was purely imitative. He declared that the little boy's action was the first sign of love because what is love if not striving to give pleasure and make someone happy?

A student of mine, Mrs. Margaret Krafft, wrote a little poem in which the behavior of her daughter Lotte, then eleven months old, is vividly described. The lines give a picture of the sudden and surprising change of the child's mood.

> *Baby-girl in rage*
> Panting, snorting,
> Jumping tall,
> Small panthercat
> In rage royal
> Claws with her
> Vigorous paw
> While floods of tears
> Invade her maw
> And flashing eyes
> Bespeak her craw.

> But the tempest
> Soon is spent;
> Bluebossom eyes
> No more are rent
> By lightning, and
> Her mouth is curled
> As a rosebud
> Not yet unfurled
> While blissfully
> She wets her world.
> Lottie sweet shouts
> "Da, da, da"
> As she sees
> Her dear papa.*

Sometimes the emotional reactions of fathers are more interesting than the actions of their little sons. Here are two incidents: a one-and-a-half year-old boy woke up in the night and cried. The father took the child, tried to calm him down and finally laid him into his, the father's, bed. But the little boy continued to cry and repeated "Mommy-bed." The father experienced the first vague emotions of jealousy. The same father was walking with his son, now two years old, in the garden of his house. He saw a place where the ground was uneven and tried to smooth the spot by trampling the earth. He was called to the telephone. While he was talking, he saw through the window of the room that his little son, left alone, was trampling the ground exactly as he had seen his father doing. The man experienced a strange feeling of relief, which he expressed in the words: "My son will once take my place; he already does my work."

Here are a few examples from the early life of my daughter Miriam. When she was not yet four years old, she climbed

* Translated from the German by Noel Bustard.

up to my lap and turned to her mother teasing her: "Eh, eh, I kissed your husband!"

Two features illustrate her early perceptiveness: when she was four years old, she remarked that her mother had a "telephone-voice." She meant that her mother spoke differently when she had a conversation on the telephone than when she talked with the person directly. Perhaps a little boy might not have observed his mother so acutely. At the same age Miriam said about a lady who often visited us: "She is like a man. She always wears the same things."

When my son Arthur was a very little boy he slept in the room with a nurse. He once surprised us by telling us: "Anne also had a weeweemaker (his childhood expression for penis), but she was naughty and it was put into the stove." He must have observed that the nurse had no penis and concluded that she once had such a genital and that it was taken away from her. To the explanation of his concept: the day before his tale the little boy had incessantly blown a toy trumpet. Anne had often admonished him to stop blowing, but he continued making the noise. Finally Anne threatened him saying, "If you don't stop I'll take the trumpet and put it into the stove."

―――――

If one can trust the reports of kindergarten-teachers, little girls frequently call them "Mommy" while little boys never use this name.

―――――

A man remembers that he felt very ashamed as a little boy when he played with other children of the same block and his mother called down from the window to the street, "Murray, come and get your milk."

―――――

I had some fun with a boy four years old, whom I told that a certain tree in his parents' garden bore pieces of chewing-gum. I had bought some chewing gum and had hung the sticks by strings on the lower bough of the tree. The boy climbed up and picked them. He did not doubt that they grew on the tree, now did he consider that they were wrapped in paper. He willingly accepted my explanation that the sticks of gum, blossoming at different times, had various flavors. In the following year when I reminded him of the chewing-gum tree, he was very ashamed of his previous credulity and said, "Don't mention that." I could not help thinking later on that ancient people are often ashamed of their previous beliefs and superstitions when they outgrow certain phases of their evolution.

Some critics of psychoanalytic theories find it hard to believe that little boys attribute in their thoughts an unlimited power to their fathers. This belief is often unconsciously preserved in later years in spite of the conscious knowledge of the fathers' limitations. I remember the great impression made on me when as a little boy I visited my father's office. I saw on his desk a number of differently colored, sharpened pencils, and I thought that my father must be a very influential and important person.

My son Arthur with whom I once went to the railway-station in Vienna where we are waiting for a relative asked me, "Daddy, make another express train come!" He attributed to me the power to make trains arrive and depart.

Little girls sometimes whisper to each other, "Men do" this or that. Little boys almost never speak of women in this way.

When my daughters were small we sometimes looked at cartoons in *The New Yorker* magazine and I asked them to explain the cartoons to me, to tell me what was funny or humorous there. I did that to test their intelligence and perceptiveness (I preferred pictures without captions). During the last war I showed my daughter Miriam, then four years old, a cartoon in which a general and his adjutant were inspecting a camp. The two officers had to pass a tent in which members of the WAC had put their laundry, panties, brassieres and so forth, on washlines. The general and his adjutant were visibly embarrassed. Miriam explained the cartoon: "These two men are ashamed because they see something they are not supposed to look at." I doubt if a boy at the same age would have understood the meaning of the cartoon so soon and, if he had, that he would have found an explanation of such delicacy of feeling.

A physician who lived in a suburb of Vienna had promised to bring his little daughter a doll from the city. Every evening she waited for her father to return home from visiting his patients. The busy doctor always forgot to buy the doll. Finally he asked his wife to buy a doll when she went out to shop. She brought the doll and gave it to the little girl. The child, full of rage, smashed the doll, throwing it against the wall. She was severely punished. The mother did not understand that the child wanted a baby from her father, not from her.

———————

A patient as he worked in his neighboring study heard his wife and his eleven-year-old daughter engaged in a long argument. He went into the room and asked what it was all about. He was told that the argument concerned the question of what kind of buttons the girl should wear on her jacket. The man wondered if such vehement and endless arguments about buttons would be imaginable between fathers and sons.

I was told of a boy who, until he was almost four years old, thought that he was called "Shut up" as other boys were called Charles or John.

The mixture of aggressive and sexual drives is an early and intimate one. Little boys, who do not know what to say to little girls, sometimes suddenly hit them, whereby the sexual character of the maltreatment is still obvious. Little girls, too, having to deal with shy boys, will occasionally go over to them and push them teasingly and playfully. The assault of the boy amounts to a substitue for a sexual pass, that of the little girl to a concealed sexual invitation in the sense: "Shall we dance?"

Children are far from feeling superior to animals and do not develop the haughtiness grownups show towards them. A little boy said he wanted to go out and visit "a good friend of his." I later realized that the friend was a dog on the next block. For children "son of a bitch" is no abuse. They would wonder as little about their canine ancestry as the ancient Egyptians did.

When I was on summer vacation a few years ago, I ran into a couple I knew and their little son on the main street of Bar Harbor. The husband, who saw me first, said something to his wife before they approached me. I later learned he had mentioned my book *Listening With the Third Ear*. We shook hands and chatted. The little boy looked attentively at me and walked around me looking me carefully over. His father told me later on that the child was searching for my "third ear."

A boy of nine years was asked by his father who visited him in camp if he had felt homesick, and the boy replied "No." The father then asked if the other boys felt homesick. "Only a few," said the child, "those who have dogs at home."

A mother admonished her nine-year-old daughter that she should not allow boys to kiss and caress her. The mother warned her daughter, sayings, "A girl who allows a boy to do that cheapens herself." The girl asked, "And the boy?"

Nina Katz, a six year old girl, came home from school and proudly told her father, "Two boys in school are in love with me." Mr. Katz asked, "With whom are you in love?" "With the boy who loves me most." As the twig is bent. . . .

4. Do Women Understand Men?

We take it for granted that women understand men better then men women. There is no doubt that this is the case. But do they understand men really so much better and—before all—do they understand them in all directions? Do they understand all kinds of men? How far are they impaired in their judgment and understanding by their own character and by their femininity? How far is their opinion clouded by the role they attribute to themselves in man's life? Do they, for instance, know that quite a few types of men put women, love, sex, and so on in a separate compartment that has, so to speak, no connection with their other interests, is isolated from them and kept apart from them? A woman who cooks and cleans and brings up her children, shops, dresses and undresses is rarely in her thoughts and in her emotional life separated from her husband or lover. Almost everything she does or omits to do has some reference to him. A man in his laboratory or office rarely thinks of his wife while he works. She is psychologically as distant from his thoughts as if she lived on a far-away island to which he sometimes transmitted his thoughts and feelings in moments of lessening attention during his work. He feels consciously or unconsciously as if this were a wrong thing to do, as if he had gone astray when he thinks of his wife or mistress while he works. What woman would have a guilt-feeling when she—during her occupation as typist, secretary, nurse and so on—would sometimes think of a beloved man? And what man would not have sometimes a guilt-feeling in the analogous situation?

The separation of affection and sex, so familiar to most men and so alien to most women provides a second source of misunderstanding. The average woman who recognizes that her husband or lover has an extramarital sexual experience is deeply hurt in her pride because she assumes that it means so much more to him than it often does. It is frequently not more than *"une affaire du canapé,"* to use Napoleon's expression. The decisive question is often only if there is a couch in the room or not and by no means the question of whether or not he loves the other woman. The incorrect analogy-conclusion women draw is brought about by two main factors: the place or significance women have in the thoughts of adult men and the time they, men, would like to spend with women. For most serious men woman is a "sometimes thing" and not a content of their life. Those men for whom women is the main interest in life are seldom very masculine. Napoleon, who interrupts his occupation with state-affairs in order to see a woman in Vienna to whom he says *"Deshabillez vous!"* in order to return to his work after a short time, released or agreeably weakened, is not a human monster. His attitude is in the worst case the caricature of the behavior of most mature men to women who are only sex-objects. This might sound brutal and is correct only for the extreme cases, but it is nevertheless true and character-istic for the impatience, urgency and immediacy of the sex-drive of the male animal, in contrast to the emotional atti-tude of the female towards the male.

Sex is for men often an aim by itself, for women a station on the way to something beyond sex. In the thoughts of women the road from a sexual experience to another has many non-sexual prospects. In the thoughts of men it is gen-erally the distance from one sexual satisfaction to the next.

Goethe occasionally remarked that a man who occupies himself much with woman is "spun off as the wool on the distaff."

5. FROM THE SECRET LIFE OF THE FEMALE

A woman meeting a Don Juan who wanders from one girl to another might find in herself the vague hope that he will stay with her; will only care for a single woman and will remain faithful to her. Women of this kind feel an itch to use their power to hold the man to the test. This hope is in most cases as vain as the expectation that a butterfly will re-main sitting on a flower long enough to be caught. However even butterflies are sometimes caught in this manner.

A woman looking at herself in the mirror before giving herself to a man for the first time will think: "Will he be satisfied with me when he sees me naked, with my figure, my breasts?" She is afraid he may be disappointed with her when he sees her without her clothes. No man experiences similar feelings before approaching a woman sexually.

A man made a stormy pass at a woman. She rejected him and reproached him for his impatience. He waited two days to ask her for a new date. He then renewed his efforts, but the woman said: "You gave me time to think. . . ."

Every woman fantasies how a man would propose to her, what words he would use, how he would look at her, and so on. A man will perhaps anticipate the woman's response to his proposing, but hardly her facial expression or the sound of her words.

When Plato created the myth of men and women—who were originally only half a person until they were united— he did not consider that the two halves would have different feelings in their desire to be together. In love the woman feels it is heavenly to be with the loved man and hell to be without him. He wants to be with her only intermittently. She wants to be with him all the time.

When a woman thinks "I could love him" she already loves him. She is like a chess player who hesitates to touch a figure on the board, while he has already decided his next move. But more than this: a woman has often already anticipated the next move of the male partner with whom she plays.

A woman who goes to have an abortion may feel as if she is going to her own funeral. Unconsciously women conceive of abortion as murder just as the Catholic church does. They feel as though not only the unborn child were murdered but also a part of themselves has died.

Women who have had an abortion often catch themselves many years later thinking of how old that unborn child would be, whether it would have been a girl or a boy, what he or she would be like, and so forth. Thoughts of this kind are almost never present in men. Here is another proof of the fact that all intimate relations in the life of a woman are connected with her child.

No man would think that the woman who—on account of external circumstances—has to end her pregnancy by abortion does not love him. But the thought that the man who wants her to get rid of an unborn child of his does not love her—this thought occurs to every woman.

"The more I take care of him, the more I love him." A woman who sews curtains for her lover, or who cooks his favorite dish, imagines that she is married to him and is doing domestic work for him.

Even a masculine woman takes on a new femininity when she is with the man she loves. There are some men who can make a woman feel more feminine than other men can. "He makes me feel like a queen," said a girl of a certain man.

Women, much more often than men, remember conversations they have had with the man they love, remembering not only his words but also the tone in which they were spoken.

Women often wonder why being touched by the hand of one man—for instance in being helped out of a car—is such a different sensation from being touched by the hand of another man in similar circumstances. In the one case they want to draw closer to the man, in the other they want to withdraw from him.

We say of certain men that they are lady's men. The French have the expression *"l'homme a femmes,"* which means a man who is very interested in women, but sometimes denotes a woman-chaser, a Don Juan. Men among themselves speaking of "a lady's man" often use the term in a derogatory sense as though disproving that a man's interest could be concentrated on women. To be a great lady's man means, somewhere, not to be much of a man. There are no analogous expressions applied to women. Those which are used in a similar sense concern promiscuous women and have a very coarse connotation. Nobody says: "She is a man's woman" or she is a *"femme a l'homme,"* because this would amount to an insult. Applied to women who show a great interest in men, the expression would be meaningless because interest in men is an immanent part of every woman's life. They all spend a great part of their lives in occupation or preoccupation with men: *"Cosi fan tutti."*

The lines *"Zur Liebe kann ich dich nicht zwingen, doch geb' ich dir die Freiheit nicht"* ("I can't force you to love me, but I don't grant you release") in Mozart's opera are put into the mouth of a man, but they would be more appropriate in a woman's mouth. She often cannot force a man to love her any longer, but is unwilling to give him his freedom because she hopes against hope that he will still return to his love for her.

An old experienced actress who studied the part of Juliet with a young woman interrupted the recital of her pupil at a certain passage. The young actress' concept of Juliet was that of a romantic teen-ager who was full of sentimentality. The old actress said, "Don't you know that all women— including Juliet—are mischievous?"

It is not very often that the inner objections to infidelity take a moral form with women. They express themselves rather in the shape of fear that a secret sexual affair could be found out. Carefully closed doors and pulled-down blinds sometimes are a good substitute for a clear conscience. Inner objections are sometimes raised in the name of properness, even of cleanliness. A woman would not tolerate the thought of having intercourse with her husband and then with her lover. A patient thinking of such a possibility said, "It is so messy."

French writers often describe scenes in which women in everyday conversation glide into *"confidences de femme."* These communications do not only concern concealed short-comings and handicaps of feminine life, but sometimes even details of women's intimate love-life. They are in general not said aloud, but whispered. They are often of the nature Colette once described as "Madame—how many times." There are no similar *"confidences de l'homme."* Men speak freely of their sexual experiences. They don't have so much to hide and to conceal. Not even their infidelities and weaknesses can remain hidden from women. They are, so to speak, open secrets.

That men do not understand women is sad, but their conviction that they do understand them makes men almost pathetic.

A woman who is very immature and wants to remain dependent on her mother will be unconsciously unwilling to get pregnant and become a mother. She wants to be a baby herself. Therefore she does not want to have a baby.

Youth is a charm of woman added to her others. My mother used to say "When she was young, even the witch in Hänsel and Gretl was beautiful!"

Men are not at home in the universe and therefore have to

explore it. Women who form the chain of all organic beings
are at home in the world and do not feel the urge to find out
all about it. Men have to search for things also in their own
apartment while women always know where all kinds of
objects are to be found.

The objectivity of a man often blocks a road that can only
be opened by the subjectivity of a woman. Subjectivity may
be interpreted by a man as interfering with the true statement of facts. It will often be rejected contemptuously if it
emerges in him. But he forgets that a fact becomes significant
only if related to others which he may disregard because they
don't "belong."

Woman's self-evaluation is dependent on the kind of man
who chooses her, or, better said, whom she made to choose
her. A man whose self-evaluation rises or fails with the social
position or the personal quality of the woman he chooses can
be called a man only in an anatomical sense.

Women are much more hesitant than men to declare to
their relatives that their marriage has failed. It cannot be that
they wish only to spare their family grief. Are women more
ashamed because they feel more responsible than men that
they have not made a success of their marriage?

A boy who is called a "sissy" by other boys, or by older
people, is often an object of contempt or of pity. The expression is used in a derogatory sense. There is, strictly speaking,
no corresponding word for the girl who behaves somewhat
masculine. The expression "tomboy" which comes closest to
an analogous term, is, although mostly critically applied, not
accompanied by emotional tones of scorn and pity when used
by girls towards another girl. There is even sometimes a
sound of envy heard in it.

Many women do not well understand that men need

variety in their sexual life. It is for instance difficult for a well-bred woman to comprehend how her husband can show interest in women who are sexually easy-going or even promiscuous. It is as if they refuse to admit that a person who loves Beethoven or Mozart can also like Suppé or Offenbach and can even enjoy a cheap song hit or jazz. "A pretty girl is like a melody"? Yes that's true, but this melody need not always be a refined or noble one.

To state that women appreciate compliments paid to their clothes more highly than do men is a platitude. But is it not so obvious *why* women evaluate those compliments bestowed upon their dress. Women conceive of those compliments as praise transferred from the beauty of their body. Praise for dress is thus taken as substitute for applause for the human being which the clothing covers.

Where does a man hide love letters and similar things from his wife? In books, in secret drawers of his office and so on. And women? Either among their underwear and stockings or between panties, bras, and so forth, in drawers that are taboo to men. The love secrets of women are much more intimately connected with their bodies than those of men for whom they are, so to speak, on the periphery of their lives.

A man who hears that a woman he admires is married simply acknowledges the fact. A woman who hears that a man she is interested in is married asks herself: What is his wife like? To what kind of woman is he married? If the woman does not like the man she may say, how unhappy his wife must be! A man who considers a woman very hateful will perhaps ask, as they do in Vienna, "Against whom is she married?"

Women write more letters than men, but they do not mail them as often as men. Letters written by women are sometimes destroyed and sometimes they are written only in imagination.

For a man, a tailor is a person who provides him with suits. For a woman, a dressmaker is a genius or an idiot, a master or a complete blunderer and sometimes both.

A woman speaking of a man: "I have never seen anyone who has himself so much under control as he." She meant that she was unable to arouse him sexually.

A woman says about another: "She is so selfish that she does not even experience malicious joy at the misfortunes of her best friends."

6. From the Secret Life of the Male

Highly intelligent men—even some men of genius—sometimes show an astonishing degree of dullness and insensitivity toward women's psychology. Here is a significant example: Alma Maria Mahler tells in her memories of her husband,* the world famous composer, of his behavior during the hours before the delivery of her second child. Mahler was then (June 15, 1905), forty-five years old. Early in the morning, Mrs. Mahler had felt severe pains. Her husband put on his clothes hurriedly and went out to fetch the midwife. In the following hours he did all he could to mitigate her pains . . . but the best he could think of was to read Kant to her! Mrs. Mahler sat at the writing table, writhing in agony, while the monotonous drone of his voice nearly drove her insane. "I could not," she says, "understand a word he read, and at last I could bear it no longer." She adds, in a strange understatement, that the philosophical treatise was, under the circumstances, a bad choice: it was too difficult to understand.

* Alma Maria Mahler, *Gustave Mahler*, London, 1946, p. 59.

When we put aside for the moment all other psychological factors determining the composer's behavior in that emergency situation, we are still appalled by the inconsiderateness and obtuseness of his reading to his wife Kant's highly abstract and difficult philosophical work while she is bent over in agony.

Another masculine trait, especially prevalent in young men, is competitiveness with regard to achievement and in comparison with an older man, usually a father-figure. This competitiveness will manifest itself in any field; from carpentry to art or atomic physics.

It is characteristic for young men that they choose one (or several) great men to admire and emulate as models. As long as they are very modest and cannot claim any remarkable achievements, these young men cannot imagine competing with the admired models. It is psychologically interesting that a comparison in thought between oneself and those highly respected men is unavoidable. The pattern of the relationship of the son to the father prescribed this development. Here is a representative instance: At the time of a Schubert musical Vienna was divided into two camps; those who admired Beethoven more and those who appreciated Mozart more. When Schubert was asked to which party he belonged, he answered, *"Ich bin selber aner."* The pun, almost untranslatable from Viennese dialect, means: "I am myself aner (someone)." In rejecting the suggestion that he be included in one of the two opposing groups, the otherwise modest composer not only asserted himself, but dared to compare himself with Beethoven and Mozart. To stay in the area of music: Friedrich Eckstein tells in his memories* an anecdote from

* *Alte unnennbare Tage*, Vienna and Zurich, 1936, p. 113.

the youth of Mahler. Gustav Mahler and Hugo Wolf had known each other at the Vienna Conservatory where they had both studied. Wolf told Eckstein that he ran into Mahler once on a Vienna street. Wolf pointed to a roll of notes Mahler carried under his arm and asked what he had there. Mahler said they were songs he had composed. Wolf read them there on the street and said, "Very beautiful. I like them very much." Mahler was a bit embarrassed and hesitant. Then he said: "Well, I believe that finally we have reached Mendelssohn." He meant that he had reached the most admired songwriter of his time. It is well known that Hugo Wolf, when he had become insane, stormed into Mahler's apartment many years later and declared that he was director of the Vienna opera—the position held by Mahler at the time. The wish to become director of the famous institute was one of the factors in Hugo Wolf's psychotic breakdown. (He died six years later in an insane asylum in Vienna.) In various forms, ambitious competitiveness of a similar kind appears in the fantasies of young men. More than two thousand years ago Themistocles wandered at night through the streets of Athens and declared that the laurels of Miltiades, the victor of Marathon, did not let him sleep.

The image of Gulliver who extinguishes the burning palace can have no feminine counterpart because of the anatomical difference of the urinary organs. The burning sensation in the man's urethra when he has to retain urine is rarely experienced by women. Yet it is this sensation that forms the pattern of fire and provides the model for playing with fire, often to be found with boys. There are very few arsonists amongst women. Women are in general more afraid of fire. Psychoanalytic theory asserts that that burning, urethral sensation is not only pattern-forming for interest in

fire, but has its characterological correlation in ambitious-
ness. (Don't we speak of "burning" ambition?) It seems thus
that even the comparative weakness or lack of ambition in
women is explainable by the anatomical difference of the
sexes. At first little girls sometimes try to urinate standing
like the boys, but they soon give the attempt up.

A couple on a walk along Fifth Avenue. The husband says:
"I see that I left my pocketbook at home." The wife asks:
"Didn't you remember that I wanted to buy various things
today?" "Yes, I did." Is this a slip of the tongue or a sincere
answer?

Married men are often envious of their bachelor friends
and of the freedom they enjoy. Married women feel in general rather sorry for their single girl friends and experience
a kind of superiority towards them. This does not exclude
friendship, but it has to be taken with a grain of condescen-
tion.

A reaction more prevalent in men than in women reveals
itself in the psychological significance of work and of the interruption of work. Here is a personal memory of this kind. For
many years I had been accustomed to start my psychoanalytical work with patients at nine o'clock in the morning.
One beautiful spring morning a patient canceled his appointment on account of illness. Having more than an hour at my
disposal, I decided to take a walk, and crossed Broadway,
headed for Central Park. Free from work, I felt at ease and
in a good mood. Soon afterward I became mysteriously depressed. The mood persisted and I began to follow my
thought-associations to see what was bothering me. Here it is:
Crossing Broadway, I had found myself in the midst of a
stream of men and women hurrying to their offices and other

places of work. Subways and busses were crowded. Everybody was busy reaching his destination—except myself. It was not only the feeling of being excluded or "unemployed" or un-needed which had depressed me, but also something else. Work, as we have said before, reduces social anxiety or un-conscious guilt-feeling which lives free-floating in every man's existence. I was, in contrast to the people around me, with-out work at this morning hour. This "freedom" opened, as it were, the door to that social anxiety which was otherwise lulled or quieted by my usual work. The hurrying of the people around me had brought this feeling to the surface through contrast with the surrounding world. It seems that men in general stand leisure and idleness less well than women because it awakens more guilt-feeling in them.

It is remarkable that the German poet and philosopher, Friedrich von Schiller, about a hundred and fifty years before Freud, connected work and guilt. He praised in his poem, "Die Ideale," activity that reduces the great debt of times even when one becomes old.

Remorse and regret about waste of time play a greater role in the thoughts of men than in those of women and can occasionally become fateful and tragic. A patient of mine asserted in bitter self-irony that he could write a textbook about the best ways of wasting time. Any psychiatrist knows in clinical practice many cases of men who instead of work-ing spend many hours in self-regret and accusation because they do not work. There are very few women who feel this way. In postponing their task to the next day, men then see it looming as too big and too difficult to master. In their remorse they have formed a circle whose viciousness becomes turned against themselves and does not allow them to begin the work. That circle is compelling them to waste their time, which is again followed by self-reproach, and so on. Women scarcely know those bitter reflections and act as if they had "oceans of time." The remorse about waste of time as well as of money are more severe in men because these reactions reflect the more demanding super-ego of men.

A patient called himself an "Obligation-Man," varying the title of a recent book. The tendency to incur obligations one has to fulfill seems to be widely spread amongst our college-trained males. Almost all of them are obligation-men.

The functional relation between heterosexual and homosexual attitudes appears especially clear in cases in which a disappointment in one direction has occurred. A man who experienced failure in his work (in sublimated homosexuality) turned his unconscious aggressiveness or hostility toward his girl friend. A physician who neglected something vital in the treatment of a patient shows, on coming home, a decidedly critical attitude towards his wife. His guilt-feeling operates here in the same psychological manner as if he had experienced a rejection of his wish to be acknowledged and loved by his colleagues. A frustrated ambition is another feature that will unfavorably influence a man's relations with women, as if the frustration produced an inbalance with the other sex. A woman who has had from childhood an unfulfilled craving for her mother's love, will have emotional difficulties with her husband or lover because the unconscious demand for mother's love, transferred to the spouse, will interfere with her relationship with the man.

There are, of course, other determining forces which operate in the disturbances with the one and the other sex, but the element emphasized here is a constant and potent factor. Its quality depends upon, and varies with, the unconscious or repressed hostility against the other sex. It is also remarkable that this resentment is, in most cases, not restricted to a single subject, but is extended to all members of that sex. Hamlet who longs for his deceased father, and unconsciously feels guilty toward him, attacks Ophelia: "Get thee to a nunnery." He also heaps accusations and abuses on the Queen in the scene in her closet (Act III). The increased craving for his father's love, together with his failure to prove it by the task laid upon him, makes him increasingly hostile against women. At the end he appears as a misogynist. Shakespeare's tragedies provide many proofs that the poet has intuitively recognized and anticipated an emotional law that psychoanalysis had to rediscover more than four hundred years after his death.

7. Women and Work

A wise French writer once said that one of the minor tragedies of life is that women love men, but men love work. Ignore all possible objections and qualifications for the moment and assume the sentence to be correct. Has the work of women changed the fundamental emotional difference between them and men? Clearly not. Most women do not love work for work's sake as men often seem to. Women do not love impersonal work. When they want to accomplish something, whether it is in the kitchen, the nursery or the office, they want to do it for someone; for the husband, the child, the boss, for the community. Men try to change the world around them to produce effects. They are the trail blazers of nature. Women try to preserve the ways of nature. The changes they would like to see are connected with the home and with society only as far as it concerns the home.

I was once present at an argument between men and

women in which the old battle of the sexes again rose, this time in terms of intellectual achievements. At the end a mature woman said: "We gladly admit that you men are more intelligent and accomplish many things in various fields. But we women have something more important to do. Without us mankind would be extinguished. We have to see to it that there are children in the world and that there are men and women in future generations."

If there are any changes by the transformations of the industrial and economic revolutions are they so fundamental that they alter those basic differences? The fact that nearly one out of three American workers is a woman, that there are twenty-two and a half million women in the full-time U.S. labor force must produce some psychological effects. It cannot be a matter of indifference that women have gained an enormous economic power in the last generation, that they own, for instance, millions of dollars in stocks alone. Do women win the battle of the sexes in America? Is the social and economic rise of womenhood accompanied by the decline of the American male, as some authors assert? Is it correct, what a worried psychiatrist, Dr. Irene Josselyn, stated the other day, that "we are drifting toward a social structure made of he-women and she-men"?

I assert that it is not even possible to give a general answer to such a simple question as: In which way does the working woman differ in her emotional attitude from her sister who is only a housewife and a mother? The answer is dependent on so many variables that no general statements can be made. First of all, the answer depends on the recognition of what kind of women it is who goes to work; or to put it another way, what was the woman like before she went to work? Secondly, what were the motives that made her search for work outside the home? It certainly makes a psychological difference if there were economic necessities, for instance that the income of the husband was not sufficient to support her and the children. It makes a difference if the woman is dissatisfied with her life as wife, mother and housefrau and desires another sphere of occupation or another social position. It is again a different situation when an older woman whose children are married and have left home and whose husband comes home only for dinner feels that her life is too empty and wishes to do something useful that would satisfy her ambitions. In other words it is as impossible to give a general answer to that question as to that of a little girl: "Mummy, what does a thief look like?"

It is difficult to answer the question even when we know the main motives which make the women decide to work in a factory or an office. Consider the case of a woman who has strong masculine trends in her character-structure. Will the fact that she is working as a receptionist or secretary influence her so that she becomes more feminine in her relations with her husband or lover? It is very possible that her work and the feeling of efficiency and the increase of power satisfy masculine trends; that they become channeled by and restricted to her occupation while she develops more feminine qualities at home and in company away from the office. It may happen, on the other hand, that the increased independence and the new feeling of power whets her appetite and impels her even more in the direction of masculine drives. We recognize that in the area of psychological problems quantitative factors play a great role besides and beyond the presence and force of emotional tendencies.

In trying to arrive at some insights into these problems the most appropriate point of departure is perhaps what is called the sex-role differentiation. The concept of sex-role in psychology refers to those characteristics and patterns of behavior that are typical of one sex in contrast to the other.* Psychologists agree that in our society a convergence of the two sex-roles is gradually taking place. This means that there is a greater flexibility in the sex-roles, an increasing variability and cultural diversity in what was once considered the feminine and the masculine roles. What implications and effects this changed and still changing culture pattern will have upon the relations of the sexes in the future cannot be easily predicted.

The situation in present day America is as follows: since the First World War women much more than before want to be "somebody" or "do something." But what do they mean by that? We always thought that women made their influence and importance felt at home and in society merely by being there, and need not "do something." The women who live as admirable patterns in the memory of mankind are not those who accomplish admirable things in different fields of activity, but those who were the best wives and mothers and those who by their beauty, charm and personality stimulated the best minds of their time. Madame Recamier did not feel the need "to do something," for instance, to work for the government. She was satisfied that her salon was frequented by the most important people of Europe whom she influenced in the right direction. Madame de Staël was a very famous writer and admired by many contemporaries, but she did not impress Napoleon to whom she spoke of her books and who asked her impatiently: "And how many children do you have?" There were, it is true,

* Compare the article "Sex-role Development in a Changing Culture" by Daniel G. Brown in *Psychological Bulletin*, Vol. 55, No. 4, 1958.

great queens, Victoria of Great Britain, Maria Theresia of
Austria, Katharina of Russia, but women in general work
more beneficently as powers behind the throne than on it.

It seems that there was and still is a growing dissatisfaction
in many women with their sex-role, not only in young
women, but also in those no longer so young. The other day
a young girl who attends Sarah Lawrence College complained
that the time spent at school is mainly a period of waiting
for a man. She did not deny that the girls are interested in
their studies, but she rebelled against the priority of the
prospect of engagement and marriage in the thoughts of her
friends—whether they admitted it or not. Times have
changed. Not so long ago men—and sometimes women themselves—did not believe that women were able and endowed
to do the same work as men. Max Liebermann, the famous
painter and president of the Academy of Arts in Berlin before
Hitler, once declared, "There are two kinds of women painters: the ones who want to marry and the others who also
have no talent."

One encounters such a cynical attitude but rarely nowadays. Yet the doubt remains if the incentive to work in
women, whether in the arts, science or industry, is as genuine
or as "authentic" as in men. How much of it is to be attributed to social pressure, yes, even to the tendency to impress
men; or better, a man?

In an unhealthy atmosphere of competition with men
there may grow the intense wish to be equal to him; not
only to have the same right, but also the same might. (By
the way some women want to be "more equal" to men than
others.) But women's power is different from that of men.
The same basic laws govern the phenomena of electricity and
magnetism, but the two branches of physics deal with differ-

ent properties. That morbid ambition to be like a man leads
to a contest in the sense "Everything you can do I can do
better," which is itself a manifestation of a masculine form
of competitiveness. Anatole France once said, "A woman who
insists on equality renounces her superiority."

The situation is complicated by the factor of money. Money
is a simple means of satisfying our needs, but unconsciously
it is much more: not only a symbol of power, but occasionally
also a manifestation of and sometimes a substitute for affection or love. We all know the type of rich man who gives
his wife or mistress furs and jewels and all that money can
buy instead of affection and attention. The woman sometimes feels that the one replaces the other and takes her
revenge on the man who gives her everything but his love.
She demands more and more money from him, emasculating
him—in a manner of speaking—financially. The woman who
earns much more than her mate often feels superior in our
culture-pattern in which achievement is often measured by
money.

There is another complicating factor provided by the war-
years and their psychological after-effects. Men were for a
long time, even years, only in masculine company and became
accustomed to look at things and people only from a man's
point of view—as if it were the only one possible. There is
not only something funny, but also something pathetic in
Professor Higgins' complaint: "Why can't a woman be like a
man?"

Pathetic in this sense too that many women, in a mis-
guided manner, tried to be "like a man." Fortunately for us
men they never entirely succeeded. There are, however, indications enough that they often move in this, the wrong

direction, in their professional and private lives, signs that the "masculinization of woman" is progressing.

There was the recent case of a woman government official who refused to leave her position in Washington when her husband pleaded with her to return home and to take care of him and the household. We don't know what her motives for the refusal were, but we hope that it was not ambition. The flexibility of sex-roles will, we expect, not go so far in our culture that we arrive at a feminine version of

"How could I love you, dear, so much,
Loved I not honor more?"

Yet a sentence like the lines Friedrich Nietzsche wrote: "Am I pursuing my happiness? No, I am pursuing my work" is for a woman only intellectually understandable. Emotiontionally such an attitude awakens her resistances. What can be more important than the happiness of a person?

It cannot be doubted that the fact that women work in offices and laboratories, as editors and executives, has some psychological effects. One has to differentiate between women who have a job due to financial necessity and those who go work, driven by an urge to compete with men. Some of the latter group seem to relinquish their feminine role, become strong-willed and domineering. It is as if a kind of osmosis with the man who works beside them is psychologically operating. I do not, however, believe that the masculinization of the American woman will go beyond very narrow limits. The biological and emotional divergences between the sexes are basically unchangeable and no transformations of our culture-pattern can reverse them. The declaration of woman's independence, however loudly proclaimed, is rather an intention than a fact. The housewives of Vienna used to say: "Nothing is eaten as hot as it was cooked."

8. EDUCATIONAL DIFFERENCES

Pedagogues, teachers and psychologists have often discussed the necessity or possibility of a different education for women and men. Besides and beyond this debate in academic circles, life itself has provided a divergence of educational aims for boys and for girls. As far as I can see, the differences go in two directions. The growing boy is educated to undertake certain demands that are made by the generation of fathers and father-representative figures. He has to meet certain requirements in order to become an adult member of the tribe. The education of the girl is less determined by demands made upon her than by restrictions and restraints that inhibit her sexual and aggressive impulses. Mother and other authoritative women-figures exert their influence in transforming the "tomboy" into a sweet and dutiful woman. The education to shame can be considered typical in the direction toward restraint which is insisted upon in feminine education.

The second difference can best be defined by the statement that the education of a girl, in contrast to that of a boy, shows a double onset with regard to certain elementary functions. The boy child as well as the girl child learns to perform functions such as walking, talking, standing up and eating. The boy continues to act as he did from the start. The adolescent girl has, in fact, to learn these things all over again and modify what she did before. When she reaches puberty she must be re-educated in how to walk, talk, eat and stand up graciously and in a feminine way. This means actually that she has a dual educational course, whereas the boy has only a single one. To sit pretty is natural to her but she also has to learn to sit down prettily.

Another difference in the education of the sexes is that in the decisive years the demands made on boys outweigh the restrictions to which they are subjected. In the education of girls restraints insisted upon are more important than demands they are required to meet.

PART TWO

The Swinging Pendulum

1. REIK'S LAW

To many people it seems that the behavior sciences do not deserve the honored name of science at all, due to the lack of certainty brought about by verification through experiment and prediction. There are, it has been said, so many qualifications and exceptions, so much interference by unforseen factors, that the conclusions sociologists and psychologists draw from research cannot claim to rank with those of physics and chemistry, and cannot be called laws in the sense of those sciences. Here we will, however, not go into the problem posed by methodological and similar considerations about the concept of science, but present a statement of a relation or sequence of phenomena which might be analogous to a law of physics or chemistry.

I am trying to formularize a conclusion at which I have arrived after more than forty-five years of psychoanalytic practice. First, let me point out a general fact: all of us oscillate in our emotional attitude during our whole life between attraction towards the other sex and toward our own sex; psychoanalytically speaking, between heterosexual and homosexual attitudes. Everyday experience teaches us that we are sometimes more inclined to search for the company of women and that we sometimes prefer the company of men. This oscillation is, in most cases, unconscious, but can under certain circumstances, become quite conscious.

Psychoanalytic practice can complement this general statement by adding various other insights. In general we prefer the company of the other sex, while our own sex is sought out only on certain occasions. Such preference would be characteristic for the normal emotional attitude of the mature and well-balanced individual. It is psychologically interesting that the concentration of interest on the other sex, with exclusion of all attention to the same sex, signifies that the person approaches an emotional unbalance. Let us assume that a female patient is only interested in men, never speaks of girl friends, female relatives and acquaintances. If this attitude implies an exclusion of all emotional and mental interests for women, the psychoanalyst will suspect that the patient has made an effort to keep from her own thoughts and feelings an interest which every woman experiences in members of her own sex. We would conclude that this kind of interest is suppressed, but must still be there and be effective. We conclude thus from the absence of any emotional or mental preoccupation of the patient with other women that intense unconscious or repressed drives are present, pointing in this direction. Let me use a comparison: You observe a person who looks for a long time very attentively into the right corner of a room. There are two possible reasons. The first is that he sees something remarkable or interesting in the corner. The second is that he wants to turn the attention of the persons in the room away from the left corner; that he purposely avoids looking into the left corner.

Another psychological conclusion, founded on numerous experiences in psychoanalytical practice, leads beyond this point. It has the impact and the significance of a psychological law as binding and as valid as the laws of physics and chemistry. If a person cannot get along with members of one sex, and shows consistently only hostility for them, there is operating always a suppressed inclination for the other sex. Let us assume that all the relations of a woman with men—father and other male relatives, men friends and lovers—are characterized by criticism, hostility and aggression. The conclusion is justified that there is a great amount of hidden craving for love from women (for instance from mother, sisters, friends) that has remained unsatisfied. The sources, as well as the forms, of such ungratified love-feelings can, of course, be various. There is for instance an old fixation on early love-objects, lack of response from those objects, longings for an absent or lost person, guilt-feeling toward him or her etc. A man who cannot get along with women suffers from an unfulfilled desire to be loved by a man or by men. Brought to a formula, the analytic insight can be thus stated: *the degree of hostility experienced against one sex is functionally related to the degree of ungratified unconscious love for the other.* This unsatisfied craving can under certain circumstances become conscious, but may remain repressed. The importance of the functional relation between hostility against one sex and the lack of satisfied love for the other is not yet always therapeutically recognized. The relation is as lawful as the functional interdependence between two numbers in an equation, and scarcely allows any exceptions. My students who attempt to verify this functional relation in analytic practice speak of it as Reik's law.

2. Who's Who in Sex?

The time when sexual matters were not discussed in mixed company have long passed, and that is good. There is an old anecdote about the wife who asked her husband before going to bed, "Will you want to use me tonight?" Women today not only freely admit that they too desire sexual pleasure, but sometimes even feel guilty when they cannot reach a sexual climax, guilty towards their partner. Recently a courageous woman, Maxine Davis, published a book under the title *The Sexual Responsibility of Woman*.* Ask any man and he will tell you that the response of the woman is important for his satisfaction, but scarcely any man dares to think that the woman—and the woman alone—is responsible for success and failure in sexual intercourse. Men have always had a vague feeling that women can contribute to this success. It was, however, a kind of superstitious belief in the magical power of the woman, somewhat in the sense of that French proverb: "*Ce qu'est veut la femme, Dieu le veut.*" She could, he suspected, be sometimes made responsible for failure in the act, but he almost never thought that he owed his success in this sphere to her. If we can believe Mrs. Davis, woman is now ready to take the leading role in this area too. What is sauce for the goose has to be sauce for the gander.

We must not forget that some men like the woman to take the active role in sex. I had a patient, a middle-aged man, who insisted that the woman should seduce him. She had to take the position usually reserved for the male in sexual intercourse and make all his movements. When I asked him why he refused to take the sexual role of the male, he replied, "That's no activity for a gentleman."

But we will not consider semi-pathological cases of this kind, but rather the woman's role as it is heralded in a few recent books on the subject. It is only a step from the stage reached here to a phase where the woman takes the sexual

* New York, 1956.

initiative. ("Won't you come into my parlor, said the spider to the fly.") The leading role attributed to woman is not restricted to general behavior, but sometimes concerns the details of technique of sexual intercourse for whose success she is made responsible. Maxine Davis prescribes, for instance, how the woman should behave in the moments before the sexual climax of the male. To quote from her book, she "must let her husband know exactly how she is reacting. He can arrive at his orgasm at any moment now. He needs to be cued in his actions to help her reach hers with him. He can delay ejaculation by mental control, by directing his thoughts towards something else for a few minutes or by lying quietly. . . ."

I assert that the mental control here recommended is really that which the woman wants to exert over the sexual partner. I assert further that the advice here given is utterly bad because it is founded on a false concept of man's sexual life. Man can postpone his emission to a certain extent and does so to make up for what Freud once called the difference of phase in the excitability of man and woman. When, however, his excitement has reached a certain point, a point of no return, delay would be harmful not only to himself, but also to his sexual partner. Any delay might then result in premature and unpleasurable emission for him and disappointment for her. Human nature is not made to submit to great sacrifices.

It seems to us that women in general like the man to take the initiative in sexuality. The initiative has to be his—at least officially. If we could imagine that advice as here quoted was followed consistently, the consequences would be disastrous. Woman would perhaps win the battle of the sexes, but certainly lose the war.

3. Ambition and Homosexuality

There is originally no conflict in the child between love
for the mother and for the father. The two emotional interests clash only under the influence of the emerging Oedipus-
situation in which the father appears as the rival of the little
boy in being loved by the mother. It is obvious that this
situation provides a powerful component in the formation
of ambitious drives striving to reach and to replace the father.
There is, however, another emotional factor in the emergence
and development of ambition, a factor not sufficiently appreciated by psychoanalysts, namely the relation of ambition to
passive homosexuality.

The aim of ambition originally is to be approved, acknowledged and admired by the parents. The little boy wants to be
praised by his mother and father, to be loved for his accomplishments. Later on the circle of people whose admiration
he seeks, will be widened and will include the teachers and
playmates of the boy, later on the friends and acquaintances
and so on. Finally public opinion will take the place which the
parents originally had alone: the man wants to be famous
and appreciated by his city, the nation and by all nations.
The origin of ambitious urges in searching for the approval
of the parents remains, however, indelible and determines the
scope and character of the man's aspiration. It is, it seems to
me, the difference in the development of the Oedipus-situation, particularly the minor intensity of aggressive drives,
which decides the fact that ambition is not as strong in women
as in men. Vanity and pride of her beauty will be the equiva-
lent of masculine ambition to the woman.

The neglected emotional factor in the psychological analysis of ambition is the unconscious homosexual relationship

with the father. Not only will competitive tendencies be operating in the development of the boy's aspiration; the father will be unconsciously an admired object. Besides the continuation of love and admiration for father, another trend will develop as a product of the Oedipus-situation. As an emotional reaction to the impulses to remove and to replace father unconscious guilt-feelings will evolve whose depth will be the greater the more intensively the aggressive or even murderous wishes are experienced. This reactive guilt-feeling tends in the direction of atoning for those hostile impulses and manifests itself as a need to honor the father and to be forgiven by him. Those unconscious feelings enter the realm of ambitious strivings and intensify their emotional power. The creative function of unconscious guilt-feelings is proved by the achievement of the son, by his accomplishments. These accomplishments simultaneously show that he has become victorious over his father, and that he honors the memory of the still powerful father. The unconscious aim of ambition is thus on one side to overcome and surpass father, on the other side to offer him proof of one's love and admiration for him. The intensity of unconscious guilt-feelings, operating in ambition, is determined by the need to be loved again as in childhood, to be approved by the father and to undo the deed aimed at his destruction. The continuation of those imperative strivings can be traced by analysis to the repressed wish to offer oneself as a love and sexual object to the father whose forgiveness is searched. In this way ambition which is consciously akin to competitiveness and aggression has also unconscious roots in a passive feminine homosexual attitude.

The discovery of a hidden agency of a passive, feminine homosexual trend within ambitious drive is, of course, founded on clinical experiences in psychoanalytic practice.

Here is a representative example which I present in a slightly changed form, owing to reasons of discretion: a young, very ambitious archaeologist who is digging in Greece with some success daydreams that he will discover some highly important archaeological treasures. He sees himself in his fantasies being celebrated and praised by Professor X, the famous and admired old master of classical archaeology. This old man cordially shakes his hand and affectionately congratulates him. The train of associative thoughts lead the young scholar to a contrast between American and French customs. He emphasizes that in France at such occasions the superior man, celebrating the younger man's accomplishments, would embrace and kiss him. In Anglo-Saxon civilization the "accolade" is not performed. The young archaeologist, imagining such a scene enjoys the affection of the master and gets much satisfaction from his fantasy. He says that he is very fond of the old man, who is to him an elevated father-representative personality. Then the question emerges in the patient if he would perhaps wish to be sexually used by the old archaeologist, a question which is most energetically answered in the negative. His thought-associations touched at this point the repressed passive homosexual tendencies, which were consciously energetically rejected.

4. FANTASY AND REALITY

Many sexual things are allowed and enjoyed in fantasy, while they are forbidden in reality. Fantasy belongs to the realm of fore-lust phenomena and is characterized by pleasurable suspense. Often unconscious prohibitions and sometimes conventional considerations prevent fantasies from transgressing into the realm of reality.

A young girl awaiting her boy friend imagines that she will receive him with kisses and passionate caresses. When he arrives, she feels as if she were frozen. Often what is allowed in fantasy is not allowed in reality. One of the most effective emotional factors within the fore-lust is the suspense. Let us assume that a masochist gets sexually aroused by a fantasy in which he is slapped by a tall and fat woman. He often masturbates with this fantasy and experiences an orgasm. Now let us assume that this same man when walking on a street is attacked by a woman who belongs to that Brunhilde type. Let us further assume that she has confused him with another man who had wronged her. She slaps the face of the surprised masochist. Will he experience any pleasurable sensation or sexual excitement? This is very unlikely. It is more probable that he will be indignant and full of rage. The development of suspense as a condition necessary for the sexual arousal is lacking.

A man who had a long affair with a woman who, as he knew, had been promiscuous, married her finally when she threatened to marry another man. The new husband soon realized he had made a mistake and complained that he felt trapped and imprisoned. He could not explain to himself that his wife with whom he had had highly satisfactory sexual relations had lost all charm for him. The stimulus of the forbidden was not enough to explain his change of attitude. During his psychoanalytic treatment he had to recognize that just the promiscuity of his mistress was the determining factor in the attraction she had for him. It was this emotional undercurrent which formed a hidden bridge between him and other men, an unconscious homosexual tie with the same sex. The faithfulness of his wife diminished the sexual power she had over him. It was, he said, as if she had lost a certain "haut-goût" for him.

5. SEXUAL ROLE-PLAYING

A patient was only weakly potent with his wife and even then could function sexually only when she followed his suggestions, which were strange enough: she had to stand or sit behind him and caress his testicles from behind with one hand while she stroked the nipples of his breast with the other. It was obvious that he acted the role of a woman to whom he wanted to do that and was too shy to do it. His wife had to play vicariously the role of the aggressive man. Another case of a similar kind gave at first the impression of transvesticism. A middle-aged man was impotent with his wife except under bizarre and extraordinary circumstances. He had to dress in the clothes of his wife, including stockings and so on, and came then into the bedroom where she was lying. He caressed her and aroused her sexually. The husband acted vicariously the part of his wife. It was as if he could become potent only when the woman took the sexual initiative and brought him so far as to desire her. The man appeared in this often repeated scene in the role of the wife who invites him to have sexual intercourse because she herself desires it. The common factors of both cases are an identification with the woman and a particular shyness of the man in his sexual approach. Both features had remained unconscious to the patients.

PART THREE

Male and Female Spectacles:
A Few Side Glances

---

1. WOMEN ON LOVE-MAKING

Only psychoanalysts and gynecologists have occasion to hear what women think about the love-making of their spouses. Here are a few examples of thoughts of women about that delicate subject, thoughts which were translated into speech during psychoanalytic sessions. A woman about her husband, "Why does he think when I affectionately stroke his hair at dinner that I want to sleep with him? I want only to show him that I feel tenderness toward him—or rather 1 wish he should feel tender towards me."

A woman who wants to be caressed in a certain way will, if her wish is not fulfilled for a long time, caress her lover in this manner: she will, for instance, kiss him behind the ear if this is an erogenic zone for her. This is an indication that she does to him what she wishes he would do to her.

Most women feel that men express their love in a mechanical and matter-of-fact way. A woman said, "Men who want to make love seem to reduce all to the simple formula of sex. It is as if they offer you H_2O instead of water."

Continental wives do not often take the extramarital affairs of their husbands tragically. One has said, "A man sometimes likes to eat dinner in a restaurant, but he really prefers home cooking." A Viennese wife who knew that her husband had an extramarital affair said, full of contempt about her rival, "He can sleep with her, but he can talk only with me."

A wife who reluctantly yielded to her husband's wish to have sexual intercourse thought during the act about the dinner for tomorrow, whether she should prepare beans or peas. Her response under these circumstances was not very convincing.

Here is the secret thought of a woman whose husband, a minister, rarely approaches her sexually: "Praise the Lord and pass the admonition."

Women rarely speak during sexual intercourse. The one word men most often hear from them in this situation is an appealing one, namely, "More."

A woman described the kind of incipient sexual arousal that faded without reaching orgasm, "It was a ripple and not a wave."

A woman who had some frustrating and disappointing sexual experiences with various men, said sighingly, "These are only ghost-lovers."

Woman to husband speaking of sexual intercourse: "It is a long time since you pleased me." Compare the following anecdote. The Duchess of Marlborough (1660-1741) told a lady friend, "Today the Duke returned from the wars and pleasured me twice in his topboots."

Middle-aged housewife, who a short time ago found out that her husband was having an affair with a friend of hers, speaking of her reluctance to having sexual intercourse with him: "I prefer to have a tooth pulled."

2. LIFE IN DREAMS

Freud pointed out that the unconscious wishes that can be found as dream-forming powers after the latent contents of the dreams are deciphered come from deep recesses of the soul. He remarked that day-remnants (impressions and events of the day preceding the dream and providing material for its production) often awaken such concealed wishes which then appear fulfilled in the dream. It seems to me that too little attention has been given in psychoanalytic literature to the half-conscious wishes that emerge during the day and function as germs for deeper, often infantile desires of the dreamer. In other words the latent content of the dream is to some extent determined by germinal thoughts during the day and is also dependent on the will of the dreamer. There is a story of two little girls who used to tell each other their dreams in the morning. Anne who, had passed her third birthday, said that she never dreamed of her older sister. Trudy, six years old, was very indignant about that and said, "If you don't dream about me, I will not dream about you any more."

There was a young man who had a dream in which the decisive role of day-remnants is illustrated: the dreamer saw himself entering a barber-shop whose master smilingly received him and shook his hand. The dreamer had on the evening before the dream seen a movie *The Great Dictator* in which Charlie Chaplin acts as a barber. The dreamer had admired the artist and wished to make his acquaintance.

3. PYGMALION

Woman's sexual arousal is in general more dependent on the kind of love-making of the man than man's excitement on the behavior of the woman. In this sense every man wants to be a Pygmalion under whose hands the lifeless statue comes to animation. Although not every woman is a Galatea, the man is inclined to believe his task is similar to that of that Greek sculptor who could function as the patron of the sexually excited man. The success of that self-imposed task is more important for the self-confidence of the man than the realization of the social transformation performed by Professor Higgins in Shaw's play. It also demands greater ability of the male and the effect of the metamorphosis of a sexually cool woman into one who experiences an orgasm is deeper and emotionally more meaningful than the social change from a London flowergirl into a society-lady. Such a social transformation is not felt as something extraordinary by the woman, but the first experience of sexual fulfillment can become in her eyes almost a miracle.

4. EVIDENCE

A woman we will call Anne Brown became suspicious of her husband, who had to go on business trips during occasional weekends. He usually left the name of the hotel in the city where he could be reached in the event of an emergency. Mrs. Brown once called this hotel at noon and asked if she could speak with Mrs. Brown. The manager told her that Mr. and Mrs. Brown had just left, and asked her if he could take a message for Mrs. Brown. The wife said, "No, thank you," having confirmed her suspicion. It is unlikely that a man eager to find evidence in such a case would have thought of and applied such a method to find a confirmation of his suspicions. The kind of procedure the woman chose leads to the psychological conclusion that Mrs. Brown unconsciously identified with her rival.

5. No Surprise

Accidentally I observed the different reaction in man and woman at a surprise encounter. A young man saw a girl he knew go into a restaurant. The moment he recognized her, he jumped up from the chair, went over to her and greeted her cordially. Shortly afterward, in the same restaurant, I observed the behavior of a young woman in the same situation. A man she knew came in. She pretended not to see him and looked studiously at another table. When he greeted her, she looked up, pretending she had just noticed him. "Oh!" she said, in a surprised tone of voice, "I didn't see you! Good evening!"

6. Voices from the Ghetto

From time to time some funny sentences come to my mind that I must have heard from my grandfather when I was a boy of five or six years. It was at the time when grandfather, who was a widower, moved into our apartment. Some of these sentences, always spoken in Yiddish, made fun of women. Here are two of them: When a girl in the ghetto played hard to get, the Jews parodied her behavior by putting the words into her mouth, "Drag me, I just love to go." (In the original: "*Schlepp mich, ich geh' gern.*")

Another such joking saying, uttered by a woman, is, "Though I am homely, I love my husband nevertheless." (In Yiddish: *"Chodsh ich bin mies, hab' ich mein' Mann doch gern."*) This means, of course, an energetic denial of the experience that a woman who considers herself ugly cannot love a man because she anticipates that he will not reciprocate her romantic feelings. The woman who speaks that sentence shows an extraordinary courage and self-confidence.

7. Preview

Before a woman introduces her husband or lover to her woman friend, she looks her suspiciously and carefully over, face and body, and tries to find out her possible intentions. It is as if she wants to see her first with the eyes of the man, especially when the other woman is younger and prettier than herself. The feminine sense of hostility and jealous possessiveness will inevitably emerge in this tentative preview.

8. Changeability

I saw an advertisement of a clothing store showing the picture of an elegant woman. The caption said, "She is another woman every day." You ask yourself: "Why does she, whoever she may be, want to be another woman every day?" A man wants to be the same every day. He is consistent and does not wish to change with every sunrise or sunset. The advertisement implies that the woman in the picture has a different personality with every new dress. But the advertisement is pleonastic, because to be a woman does mean to be another person every day.

9. MASCULINE TRAITS

The rigid moral code of the cultured male leads finally to the arrogant assumption that he should not make any mistake and should become infallible. The absurdity of such an attitude becomes obvious in pathological distortion in the thoughts of obsessional characters. Their self-punishments and atonements always bring at the end their aggressive and cruel tendencies again to the surface. At the height of the defenses they have built up those repressed drives surprisingly emerge. A surgeon whom I treated was sometimes appalled and horrified by such sudden impulse during different operations he had to perform. When he wanted a certain surgical instrument and the nurse gave him another one that he could use just as well—he was compelled to think, "Now all is lost. I should put a knife in this patient's heart." Every slight mistake in performance is in many cases of this kind followed by despair, self-loathing and impulses of self-punishment. A man who in shaving removed some hairs beyond the line he had determined had the impulse: "Now that I've made this mistake, I might just as well cut my throat."

10. THE NORMAL PROTOTYPE

In cases of paranoia patients are overaware of the real or imagined impressions they make upon persons around them and interpret—often misinterpret—the words and gestures of those persons as reactions concerning themselves. From this sometimes emerge these impressions that lead the patients to ideas of reference. The normal counterpart to those pathological phenomena is the overawareness of a woman who enters a social party.

11. Cows and Bulls

Karl Kraus once wrote, "In the night all cows are dark, including the blond ones." In continuation of this ungallant comparison the differences between feminine and masculine temperaments could be pointed out: women might be comparable to cows that dully ruminate their food, but they are at least peaceful. Men are comparable to bulls that storm from time to time in blind rage into the china store of civilization.

12. Compulsion to Confess

Women who confess their infidelities to husbands are sometimes not compelled by the power of their conscience, but rather by cruel and revengeful trends. Similar motives are rarely to be found in men who confess their unfaithfulness to their wives. With women frequently one of the unconscious motives for their admission is the wish to show their husbands that they are attractive to other men. Even the hidden hope to win him back sometimes appears as a factor in their confessions.

13. Genius and Sex

Elie Metchnikoff, the great biologist (1845-1916), considered genius a secondary sexual character, like the bass voice or the beard. His theories are now obsolete. The rarity of emergence of genius among women links this fact nevertheless with the sexual characteristics. Freud declared that sexuality is essentially masculine. Would it not be appropriate to assume that genius is essentially masculine also when it appears among women?

14. FAUTE DE MIEUX

The French, who are considered a frivolous nation, have a proverb: "If you have nothing better, you sleep with your wife." (*faute de mieux, on couche avec sa femme*). Such a point of view is scarcely imaginable in women. Not on account of their greater faithfulness, but rather because the sexual object is not as easily interchangeable for women as for men. Many women would most probably not wish to sleep with their husbands, if their lover were just absent. The difficulty for them is that their sexuality is highly tied to the personality of their partner. The interchangeability of sexual objects is as possible for them as the exchange of another child for their own.

15. THE PEDAGOGUES

John Fisher once pictured a bride, looking very sweet, marching up the aisle with her man, turning her radiant face to him and whispering, "Stand a little straighter, dear!" This is the beginning of the taming of the beast, or to put it more charitably, of the long process of education of husbands many brides have anticipated in their thoughts.

16. SURPRISING QUESTION

An executive who has a suburban cottage and drives daily to his New York office told his friends that during the recent great snowstorm he was not able to return home. He could not even get any telephone-connection with his wife and decided to spend the night in his office where he made himself as comfortable as possible on a couch. One of his friends

who had attentively listened to his account of that night
asked, "Was she pretty?"

17. THE OTHER SIDE

Gretchen, in Goethe's *Faust*, thinking of her lover, wonders, "How much such a man can think and think!" It iş
remarkable that men do not experience an analogous astonishment, "How much such a woman can feel and feel!"

18. THE MIRROR

A woman asked, "Do men look into a mirror at all except
when they shave?"

A woman looking into a mirror repeated aloud the words
of tenderness a lover had spoken to her the evening before.
It is possible that a man would recall and repeat endearing
phrases his sweetheart had said to him, but it is scarcely
imaginable that he would do so while looking at himself in a
mirror.

19. THE DAUGHTER-IN-LAW

A woman frequently visited fortune-tellers, on whom she
spent a good deal of money. Once she went to a woman
who had been very much praised because she could predict
the future. The fortune-teller told her client some astonishing things about past and present experiences. But then she
began to foresee the future of Peter, the thirteen-year-old
son of the customer. She predicted that the boy would marry
a very nice girl and Peter's mother would like her very much.
"I recognized then," the future mother-in-law reported to me,

"that the woman was a phony. I paid her and left because I cannot imagine that I would like Peter's bride very much whoever she might be."

20. THE BAIT

Caresses and affectionate gestures, exchanged amongst women in the presence of men, have sometimes the significance of unconscious baits for the man. They should awaken the wish in him to be caressed in the same way.

21. LEGITIMACY

In extra-marital relations the desire of women for legitimacy comes to a manifest surface. It is not only the wish to be married but a deep-seated need for legitimacy that propels women. There are sudden resentments welling up in the woman who lives in an illicit relationship, however broad-minded she might be; an upsurge of anger, as if the man were unwilling to take her into his life to make her his own. A woman who gets a husband gains stature in the eyes of other women and loses some of it when she becomes a widow or gets divorced. Nothing comparable in the case of widowers or divorced men. They too are envied by their married men friends. Freedom is not as much enjoyed by modern woman as she now often pretends.

22. THE NEW GOYA

More than one hundred and fifty years have passed since Goya conceived the eighty-two pictures called "Les desastres de la guerra." No modern artist would dare to present the

horrors of war in our time. Human imagination was able
to invent the means of the holocaust threatening the extinc-
tion of all life on earth. But human fantasy is insufficient
to depict it in works of art. Goya resurrected would perhaps
now paint the disasters and horrors of the war between the
sexes. There are phenomena common to war and to the relations of the sexes. The ring on the finger marks for instance
the woman as victorious and the man as prisoner of war,
alimony resembles a war indemnity and children have often
been used as hostages.

A moment might come in this war when the only possible
solution would be to confront a destructive and domineering
woman with the ultimatum: "Unconditional surrender."

23. Mood and Appearance

Even in moods caused by emotional upheavals many
women remain aware of their appearance. Some, for instance, at such times, have their hair in a state of highly
cultivated disorderliness.

The writer, Karl Kraus, came on a psychological detour
to the conclusion that only a man can afford to be unhappy
in love. A woman looks in this condition so awful that her
bad luck becomes understandable.

24. Sex and Name

As if we had not enough confusion about sex, we are perplexed by a new custom: some men have feminine names and
some women have masculine names. " 'this but thy name
that is my enemy," says Juliet. "O Romeo, Romeo, wherefore
art thou Romeo?" It is a good question, but imagine how

hopelessly confused the girl would be if her lover had been called Romeo Mary Montague! People nowadays adopt several names so that one can never be sure if a person mentioned only by name is a man or a woman.

In the beginning of World War I when the Austrian poet, Rainer Maria Rilke, was inducted, a hilarious scene took place. The sergeant who jotted down the personal data of the shy writer asked him, "What's your name?" "Rainer Maria Rilke." The sergeant, bewildered and suspicious that the recruit was kidding him, shouted, "What d'ya mean? Maria! I don't call myself Mizzi."

25. Reading

A man said of his wife, "I know her as if she were a book of my library." But a book is read with different reactions by other readers. A man who uses that comparison might be mistaken in assuming that this particular book was always part of his library. Perhaps it once belonged to a lending library and has passed through many hands.

26. Protection

A patient who fought with unconscious resistances during his analysis called the analyst in his thought-associations, "the respectful prostitute." The association was determined by the fact that the patient remembered that he had on this day to give his monthly check to the analyst. The comparison of the analyst with a prostitute is not only due to the element of money to be paid, but also to the feeling of emotional release in analysis. It is significant that in a kind of unconscious projection the patient's homosexual trends are in this way transferred to the male analyst. The adjective respectful, taken from the title of Sartre's play, is not only ironical, but reflects also the reverence the patient felt for the analyst.

27. THE PLACE OF THE SEXES

The fact that man forms the center of woman's interest and that woman can claim only a place at the periphery of man's interest explains that often strange geometrical configurations appear in the view of an observer of the relations of the sexes. The most common form is, of course, that of a triangle.

28. THE CONSPIRACY

Certain men sometimes have the impression that women at a social party or at other occasions "gang up against" them; that they have means and methods of secret communication among themselves. There are, these men assert, certain glances over the shoulders of the men, certain smiles and amused gestures from one woman to the other. There is even a kind of "conspirational whisper."

PART FOUR

The Strong and/or The Silent

1. Talk and Silence

No one ever speaks of a strong, silent woman. Some women are strong, but they are not silent. Speech is not only communication, but also an expression of a friendly attitude. Not to be on speaking terms with someone means absence of those social feelings. Women often—and instinctively correctly—feel that the silence of their husbands means not only indifference or lack of affection, but hostility. They experience it as rejection. A patient in psychoanalysis who is fond of Harry Belafonte's records complained that her husband never says anything about them when she puts the records on. She is right. He does not like them.

A lawyer complained that the people with whom he had to negotiate talk a lot of irrelevant, utterly unimportant things. It wearied him that he had to listen to and take part in such conversations in which unessential trifles were discussed. His wife complained that he rarely talked to her and restricted his speaking to the necessary. He had no gift for small talk and felt it necessary to speak to the point, and to focus on one subject. He did not understand that talking with his wife had not only the function to communicate certain things, but was also an expression of affectionate feelings and that talking about irrelevant things in situations, in which he had to carry on negotiations, fulfilled also the social function of getting acquainted with others—an important premise, often facilitating and smoothing the business-discussions. There is a proverb which says, "By speaking together people come together," meaning they get along better.

The fact that women are much more talkative than men can be traced back to the evolution of the two sexes according to which theory a woman retains much more of the emotional character traits of the child than the man. It is not—as some mysogynous men assert—that she is scatter-brained, but rather that it is difficult for her not to vocalize the unessential, to exclude the marginal thoughts or peripheral impressions from articulation. But how can this feminine, or, if you prefer, childlike attitude be brought in line with the acknowledgment of her ability to keep certain things secret? It is well known that she can keep things to herself much better than a man if she really wants to. The contradiction can be removed by assuming that her mental and psychological development moves on two separate tracks. In one she remains childlike and her evolution remains behind that of the male, in another she is way ahead of him and is more mature and adult than he. We could also add that a woman who wishes to conceal something is by no means silent. Many women are especially talkative when they are anxious. Men rarely are. Sometimes a woman projects her own emotional reactions onto the man and feels he is cross with her when he is only silent or thoughtful.

Sacha Guitry once said that there are people who talk until they find something to say. There are quite a few men who belong to this group. There are women who talk until they find something not to say and then they talk more.

The nicest words a woman likes to hear from a man are, "I love you." The nicest words a man likes to hear from a woman are, "I am so proud of you."

2. SILENCE AND TALK

It is still valid that a man is attracted to a woman by her appearance and personality. Even women who are sure of their beauty often doubt that a man will be lastingly interested in them; that they have nothing to offer the man but their personal charms. Much more often than men, women fear they are boring. (Men do not fear this. It is possible for them to be quite boring without the slightest realization of it). Women sometimes fear that they have only "small talk" to offer. This fear can lead them to saying quite silly things, or to being actually tongue-tied. Men in their masculine conceit are led to believe that a woman would be interested in their construction business or their political opinions, in labor troubles or difficulties in management and organization. Most women aren't, but they pretend to be. Besides that, they know that the man, in speaking of these various subjects, reveals the kind of man he is and this—not the issue discussed—interests them. Men do not fear being boring, because they can always court the woman and flirt with her. Also a woman who is afraid she could be boring to a man has excellent means at her disposal to appear interesting to him. She needs only ask the proper questions about him, about his business and his other interests. In making the man talk about himself she often has found a way to appear not only interesting, but also very intelligent.

A man may be painfully aware that he has no "small talk" and a woman may fear that she has only "small talk."

As a problem of social education emerges, the acquirement of two different abilities for man and woman in company becomes obvious: that the woman learns to be silent while her inclination is to talk and that the man learns to talk while his inclination is to be silent.

Men have a tendency to devaluate the meaning of words and show thus a revolutionary tendency. Think for instance of the word maiden, that meant originally only virgin. It means today only a female servant, not necessarily virginal. The French word fille (originally young girl) is today synonymous to prostitute. There is no comparable tendency of devaluation of words in women's society. A woman can say to a man offensive and flattering things. A man can say to a woman flatteringly offensive and offensively flattering things.

We are too little astonished by two facets of women's conversation. When we consider how many subjects are avoided in their talk, we are not enough impressed by the fact that women are in general more communicative than men. Those avoidances have not the effect of making women silent, but only more able to paraphrase things. Although women's emotional reactions are more immediate than those of men and their expressions are restricted by social considerations and conventions, it is almost impossible to find a woman who is "tongue-tied."

Young analysts have to learn how powerful silence is. The temptation to say everything one has learned to understand and to tell the patient what he has unconsciously revealed is for them often irresistible. Yet they have to learn to wait until the appropriate moment arrives to speak. The timing of speaking is announced by an unconscious and repeated signal within the psychoanalyst. One needs not raise a net immediately when one knows one has caught a fish. You had better wait until you know what you have netted before you pull the draught out from the depth. The power of silence is a double one: exercised on the patient it operates as a bait, asks him to speak, to answer an unspoken question. But it works also on the psychoanalyst who gets some satisfaction from his own restraint, from his ability to keep silent while he feels tempted to tell what he has guessed or recognized. Knowledge is power, especially when it is not yet shared with the other person, but will be conveyed at the proper time.

The self-confidence or the ego-strength of a person might be reduced by many factors for instance by the recognition of one's defenselessness or powerlessness, by inadequacy-feeling, illness and so on. One of the most serious factors impairing the strength of the ego is unconscious guilt-feeling. An oversevere conscience frightens and terrifies the person. "Thus conscience doth make cowards of us all." One of the most important tasks of the psychoanalyst is to strengthen the self-confidence of his neurotic patients by reducing the demands of a too severe superego and to accept himself. This difficult task must be approached also in convincing the patient that he has kindness besides hostility, love besides hate and helpfulness besides maliciousness. He needs to be encouraged in the spirit of that device of the seigneurs de Gruuthuus of Bruges: "Plus est en vous." ("There is more in you than you think.")

3. Telephone Conversation at 12:30 A.M.
An Example—Slightly Unfair?

"Hello, hello, is this the police? This is Mrs. Margaret Wolff speaking at 426 East End Avenue. . . . Yes, that's near 79th Street. I need help! Four weeks ago some new people moved into this apartment house. They start to play the radio or TV every day after eleven at night. Very loud too. I just can't sleep at all. . . . What did you say? You are the Missing Persons Bureau? How did I get that number? Oh, I see. . . . What precinct should I call? Are you sure they will take care of me? Just a minute while I get a pencil. . . .

"Hello, is this the police? I have a complaint. Please help me! I haven't slept for four weeks [then follows the description as before]. . . . My husband? I am a widow. . . . Yes, of course I went to the landlord, but he just had a great calamity in the family. His daughter had an accident when she drove her child to school. She is in the hospital, so of course he doesn't pay much attention to what goes on in the apartment house now. . . . The superintendent, you say? Yes, of course, I have been to him several times to complain. Only yesterday I went to him again and told him I could not sleep! Those people begin to play every night after eleven o'clock. . . . Calypso and jazz. . . . It drives me crazy and I am really quite sick. Please do something! What do you say? I should speak to the superintendent? He is really a mean man. He promises he will find out who it is and never keeps his promise. . . . It is very loud and they play until two or three in the morning. The superintendent won't do a thing unless you tip him well. . . . Of course I give him something at Christmas time, and whenever he repairs something in the apartment. I give him a dollar, at least. Yes, this is Mrs. Margaret Wolff. . . . Apartment B. . . . Yes. That's near 79th Street. Will you please forbid those people to play so late and so loud in the night? If they would at least turn it down! I haven't slept in four weeks. . . . Of course I do! I shout at them from the kitchen window, but do they pay any attention? No! It goes on and on! If you wait a minute, I'll let you hear it on the

phone. Did you hear that? No? No, they haven't got a telephone. . . . Well, wait until you get over here. You'll hear!
Yes, apartment B. Thank you!"

Half an hour later, the bell rings and a young policeman
enters. "Did you make a complaint about someone playing
the radio too loud, lady?"

"Yes, but I don't know if it's the radio or the TV. It goes
on and on until morning . . . I can't sleep at all . . . it's so
loud, it sounds as if it were in this room! Now, I don't hear
it. They have stopped. But if you wait a while, you will hear
it. . . . I shouted down at them, but to no avail. I told the
landlord but he has trouble in his family. His daughter had
an accident in her car while she was driving her child to
school. The poor man has his troubles so he just doesn't pay
much attention to the apartment house anymore. I asked the
superintendent to speak to those people, but he doesn't pay
any attention to me. You have no idea how mean this man
is! He only cares about how much money you give him. I
assure you I give him plenty when he repairs something for
me. . . ."

"Where do these people who are bothering you live?"

"Where do they live? I don't know! Perhaps over there on
the other side. The landlord asked me that too, and so did
the superintendent. I don't know such things! Perhaps they
are in the adjoining house. But even if they don't live in
this house, I tell you it is as loud as if it were in this very
room! Now they have stopped, but if you wait a while, they
will begin again. How should I know where they live? It's
for you to find out!"

"But, lady, I can't just go from door to door and ask who
played the radio or TV after eleven o'clock!"

"Why not?"

"Look, you're not even sure if it's in this building or not! Don't you think you'd better find out where the noise is coming from? Then go and talk to the landlord or the superintendent. I'm sorry, but I can't help you. Good night!"

4. WHAT MEN SAY ABOUT WIVES

A physicist speaking of his marriage used scientific terms describing its character. He said that his moods are a function of distance. He meant he felt in a good mood the further away he was from his wife. The same patient differentiated between his life at the office and that with his wife and children. He called the latter "the homefront." Once on leaving his office to go home he thought: "Now begins my night shift."

A man ruminated: "Why is there no insurance to cover the possibility of marriage, as in the case of other accidents? I'm sure experts would find that there are men who are marriage-prone."

A patient spoke of the different ways of leaving women with whom he had an affair and said, "I am departing from her this time, not escaping as in other cases and that makes a lot of difference. When you escape, you carry remnants of chains with you, but when you depart you have said 'good-bye' to a period of your life."

Another patient who was married and had an affair with a divorced woman described the evening he had spent with his mistress: "She is not stupid. As a matter of fact she is quite intelligent and after dinner she spoke of a book she had read, but I was not interested in what she was saying. I was listening only with half an ear. I was thinking the whole time of making love to her and I began to caress her and say sweet things to her, but in reality I wanted only to go to bed with her as quickly as possible. Mind you, I am not a calculating seducer. I was even temporarily sincere in what I was telling her. My desire is so strong that I sometimes confuse it with love, but I know, of course, that I don't love her. Immediately after sexual gratification I feel rather repelled, but she is then tender and speaks in terms of love. That's a long way from what I feel. Whenever she speaks of herself and me as 'we,' I flinch. I am then even less interested in what she says than before sexual intercourse and sometimes I am tempted to say to her, 'Stop inflicting your personality on me!' Yet I acted before as if I loved her. I am aware of my duplicity and of my playing a part, but I can't help it. At the end I always ask myself, 'Is it worth it?' Yet I know that in five or six days, with the new onset of sexual desire and when I am overwrought with tension, I will want her again. I only know I don't love her."

A man who is interested in Greek mythology sometimes uses comparisons from this area for his married life: "When I married her, I was as unaware of the dangers I secured for myself as the Trojans who brought a wooden horse filled with enemies into their city." Sexual intercourse with his wife appeared to him as vain as the work of Danaides who had to fill a barrel full of holes with water. He compared his love-life before he had married with the free flying of an eagle while he now appears to himself rather as a bird with clipped wings.

A husband about his wife, "She is like the Director of Internal Revenue. The more I earn, the more and the more unfair become her demands."

A seducer speaks, "The best way to get a woman is to be

first extremely gentle and considerate to her and then when the moment comes, to move in with strength and force."

5. TELEPHONE CONVERSATIONS

A man who happens to witness the telephone conversation of his wife with a lady friend is often subjected to delusions which only insane persons have otherwise. He might be compelled to think that he is the victim of an endurance test and the subject of a torture compared with which the martyrdom of some Christian saints pale into insignificance. He might be overwhelmed by the impressions that an abundance of trifling and unessential things are purposely invented in order to be broadly and in detail discussed in the telephone conversation.

If he happens to be a psychologist, he has here plenty of opportunity to re-examine several problems of his science, for instance the difference between objective and subjective time measurements. When he expects for instance a very important call from Los Angeles, he can by way of introspection observe how his "frustration-threshold" sinks more and more, the longer he listens to the conversation between his wife and her friend. The time spent in which the two ladies discuss the party of yesterday appears to him then as eternity while in reality only a few hours have elapsed since the conversation started.

Telephone conversations are for most men communications; for most women social encounters and often visits with all traits of such except the visual ones. Some men fear that some modern device may be found to complement the telephone with simultaneous pictures of the speakers—a sort of combination of telephone and TV. Thus the telephone visit a woman pays to another would be complete and the telephone connection would become the life line of modern woman.

6. On a Certain Awareness

They say that it is characteristic of a gentleman that he is never rude—except on purpose. This attitude is the result of tradition and the outcome of a definite social education. We all know that this fails to be true in moments of intense emotion. Then—and perhaps not only then—even a gentleman is rude without intending to be. More important and decisive for the emotional differences of the sexes is the question of whether the man is aware of the hurt which he has inflicted by his rudeness to another person. I feel that men very often remain unaware that they have hurt someone's pride or embarrassed him by some remark, little action or faux pas. This, however, is extremely rare with women. Women, occasionally, can be as rude as men, but the woman who would be unaware of the hurt she has inflicted would be likely to be either a psychopathic person or a freak of female nature. This is valid for all women and is not dependent upon her milieu nor upon the degree or character of social education. In other words, this awareness or sensitivity is a quality to women of all walks of life—common to the duchess and to the fishwife at the market.

7. Tyranny of Mothers

In the general and to the greatest extent justified praise of motherhood we too easily forget that some mothers exert a severe tyranny upon their children. Those mothers are rarely aware of some bad effects of their behavior and often deceive themselves about their role in the life of their daughters and sons. There is, for instance, the almost invisible tyranny through pity. Often sick women use this emotion as an attention-getting instrument. An older woman used to complain every time her adult son visited her about her various illnesses and pains to reassure herself of his care and compassion. The son was so accustomed to his mother's complaints that he was almost astonished when he once visited his mother and she answered his question as to how she felt "regretfully," as he reported, "Quite well." A woman who has remained single complained about her mother with whom she lived and with whom she could not get along. She described her mother as gentle and easygoing and accused herself as responsible for the frequent conflicts in their home. The psychiatrist who treated this patient had occasion to study the attitude of the mother who once came to consult him. He had to recognize that the picture the daughter had given him of the mother was utterly false. The woman was of extraordinary strength of will and knew how to carry her will through. The psychiatrist gave a summary of the impressions he had from the mother in the sentence, "That's not a woman, that is a steamroller."

8. What They Say in Psychoanalytic Sessions

A young girl: "After I had all those drinks, I said a few off-color things. When the men laughed and looked at me, I acted the part of utter naïveté. I blushed and covered my face with both hands. I was just darling."

The same college girl: "It was a close call. He got so passionate. I said: 'Why can't we just sit and talk?' But he was not interested in my ideas and feelings. He wanted only one thing. My girl-friend says that all men are like that. . . . When I said that I did not want just sex, he asked: 'But why did you come then?' I told him that we had better not see each other any more. Then he wrote me. I didn't answer his letter in which he asked me for another date. I knew it would be just the same thing over again. But . . . you see, the real reason I didn't answer him was because I thought that, that way, he might come up from Willington to see me again. . . ."

A middle aged woman: "Now I'll tell you something catty about Mrs. Brown. Do you know what pearl shorteners are? They are small clasps designed to shorten long strings of pearls. They look much alike and are usually cheap—from eighty cents to two dollars. At a party the other day, I said to Mrs. Brown, 'What on earth are you wearing there?' She wore two pearl shorteners on a lapel as though they were jewelry. 'Oh, these?' she said. 'They are two pins a woman friend gave me the other day as a present.' "

Most men would see in this tale nothing detrimental toward Mrs. Brown. Some women might also agree, but it appears that many women would find this amusing and rather belittling. They would tell it to each other with some malice and joy—something a man cannot feel when he listens to the account.

"My husband said: 'Let's not argue, dear.' I answered, of course, 'I didn't argue. I was just sitting here. You started to argue. You came in and said. . . .' "

Young girl, Bennington student: "Susie eats like a horse and remains slim while I have to widen my waistline when I eat some icecream after dinner. I look at her how she shovels it in and I could strangle her."

A working woman: "I think he is impossible and I should not waste my time with him. I should not even think about him. There is nothing to him and I don't care about him at all. I was only curious if he will wait for me when I will come out from the office at five o'clock. The time passed very slowly."

Another girl about her friend: "Sue tries to mow them down with her charm. Whenever she is with a man, she draws him out and asks him about himself. When he tries to ask about her, she demurely says: 'Oh, don't lets talk about me! Tell me, instead, all about you.' Mind you, it isn't even done with subtlety or skill. It's just an obvious act. But it works . . . a hundred percent."

A woman: "I had that terrible dress on . . . and those darned shoes—the heels were neither high enough nor low enough, the in-between kind old ladies wear. I felt so badly dressed, such a misfit, that I drank four glasses of champagne and behaved like a fool. I talked all the time!"

A wife about her husband and a rival: "The calamity is not only that he loves her, but that she is in love with him. I don't want another woman to love him."

A society lady: "We talked about men and she said that Mr. Goudener is a gentleman, but has a lack of energy. That means, of course, that he pays too little attention to her. . . . The countess of Warenburg got engaged to Douglas Harvey, *autrefois* David Hamburger. He is very intelligent, a rich banker, but awfully Jewish. . . ."

A secretary about another: "Jane has two bosses at her office. She often comes home very late and, I guess, one of the bosses takes her to dinner. She is cooperative with both of them. Very cooperative. . . ."

A middle-aged woman tells me about a visit with her friend:

"It was really disgusting how that woman fed her husband. Would you believe it? She put one cherry after the other into his mouth. I was curious if she would let him spit out the pits himself."

A young girl about her roommate: "She does not pick up her things and she does not clean the bathtub and the room is a pig-sty when she leaves for the office in the morning. I always say: 'If there has to be a roommate, let it be at least a man.'"

A middle-aged woman about another: "She is a very vicious person and I am afraid of her. I am extremely polite to her."

A patient said: "Our marriage was the union of two desperados."

A patient said: "The death of my father makes me acutely aware that I am mortal."

Here is an instance of the contrast of a characteristic attitude during two successive psychoanalytic sessions. A man patient said: "I feel like crying, but I hate to appear weak before you." A woman: "I want to cry, but I am ugly when I cry."

PART FIVE

Sterner Moods

---

1. ON THE PSYCHOLOGY OF GUILT FEELINGS

We have still much to learn about the properties and effects of unconscious guilt-feelings. Even their origins are still in darkness. There is, for instance, the psychological fact that self-sabotage or self-punishment and conscious guilt-feelings rarely coexist. That means that when the one is efficient, the other is not experienced to a great extent. There are, of course, cases when—at least temporarily—the one lives in the shadow of the other, but this coexistence is restricted in time and effect and at the end one part of the pair becomes victorious. For the analyst often the task is given to transform self-damaging and self-punishing tendencies into conscious guilt-feeling since they are manifestations of an unconscious urge for atonement and penalty. The necessity of such a transformation results from the fact that the unconscious agency that shows itself in spoiling one's chances, manufacturing accidents and other self-damaging events and effecting severe privations in work and pleasure and so on is mute. It can only be dealt with when it has become conscious as manifest guilt-feeling together with its motives.

Another factor in the establishment of unconscious guilt-feeling is the perception that one had been especially favored by destiny in contrast to others who are dear and near to us. This kind of subterranean guilt-feeling is, of course, of various kinds and degrees, according to its underlying reasons. It can express itself as a kind of malaise, or vague discomfort, for instance in the case of the financially privileged. (Not long ago a book with the title *The Conscience of the Rich* was published.)

On the other hand it can take the form of serious self-punishment. It is interesting that it often emerges in the individual as a moral reaction to a moment of intense gratification about one's own better fortune or about one's own privileged situation compared with that of others. In some cases this reaction occurred after a person had experienced a moment of satisfaction about the death of a loved person.

Here are two examples from analytic practice, the one concerning a woman, the second a man. The first patient was a woman in her middle forties who appeared in my consultation in a mourning dress, black veil and so on. I asked her why she wore mourning. She answered that she had lost her fifteen year old son by death. To my astonishment I heard that the boy had died three years ago. The story as she reported it in analytic treatment later on was tragic indeed. The adolescent boy had a brain tumor and became insane. He often destroyed furniture and threatened people with violence. Once, left alone for a short time, he cut all the dresses of his mother to pieces. The mother refused to put the boy into a hospital because she did not wish to be separated from the beloved child. Finally he had to be put into an insane asylum. The mother was told that he was incurable. Some weeks later the boy had escaped his attendant and had hanged himself on a tree in the garden of the institution. The mother was told by telephone that the patient had committed suicide. From then on began a period of pathological mourning. She avoided her friends and was never seen except in deep mourning dress.

During the analytic process the course of inner development of her disturbance could well be reconstructed. At the moment when she heard from the director of the insane-asylum about the suicide of the son who was doomed she must have had experienced a feeling of utter redemption in the sense of "God be thanked, it is over!"

This feeling, so humanly understandable, came immediately in conflict with her great love for her son and with her moral convictions. It was energetically suppressed and had become entirely unconscious. The moral reaction that followed the emergence of that feeling manifested itself in the pathological mourning and in nervous symptoms like headaches and others.

Here is another case, concerning a man. This man, a Dutch Jew, went into hiding when the Nazis overran Holland. He lived underground with a gentile family who protected him. He recognized clearly the danger which he was in, but his younger sister who was married to a gentile man, disavowed it. He tried to convince her that she had to go into hiding and pleaded with her to follow him. She did not wish to leave her husband. In the last conversation he had with her he did his best to persuade her to bring herself into safety, but in vain. Soon afterwards the Gestapo arrested the sister who was brought into a concentration camp and later killed by the Nazis. During psychoanalysis it became transparent what the patient had experienced in the moment when he first heard of the arrest of his sister: a surprising feeling of triumph. It was as if he felt satisfaction that it was she and not he who had been taken away by the Gestapo.

The analytic process made it clear that some feelings of sibling rivalry from childhood on and other emotions were determining factors in the formation of the ambivalent attitude towards the young girl. There was even—in spite of sincere and deep grief—a kind of satisfaction in the fact that he had been right and she wrong in judging the dangers of the situation. It was, so to speak, a posthumous "I told you so." Later other emotions connected with that last conversation came to the surface. He asked himself if he had been convincing enough when he had talked with her and said, "It is now as if I then had her life and death in my hands." He himself escaped the Nazis, but for many years showed serious symptoms of self-sabotage and self-privation whose connections with the emotions at the death of his sister had remained unconscious to him. Also in this case these symptomatic traits had the character of unconscious moral reactions following the emergence of a very short-lived feeling of gratification that was violently rejected. Psychoanalysis could free him from the burden of an unconscious guilt-feeling that had accompanied him, but only after it became clear to him that his life had remained in the shadow of a sense of satisfaction that had emerged just for a moment from deep recesses.

The self-confidence or the ego-strength of a person might be reduced by many factors for instance by the recognition of one's defenselessness or powerlessness, by inadequacy-feeling, illness and so on. One of the most serious factors impairing the strength of the ego is unconscious guilt-feeling. An oversevere conscience frightens and terrifies the person. "Thus conscience doth make cowards of us all." One of the most important tasks of the psychoanalyst is to strengthen the self-confidence of his neurotic patients by reducing the demands of a too severe superego and to accept himself. This difficult task must be approached also in convincing the patient that he has kindness besides hostility, love besides hate and helpfulness besides maliciousness.

2. THE CHALLENGE OF SELF-SUFFICIENCY

There are scarcely any large regions unexplored on this our planet and the areas still blank are to be found within men, not around him, in his mind and not in his environment. It is for instance astonishing that we still do not know enough about the emotional powers that govern the attraction between the sexes. That means that there are still undiscovered strands to be found and to be isolated operating in this direction. There are still unknown or at least unrecognized essential components within the forces pulling women to men and men to women. In the following attempt at isolation and description of one of the components of this attraction my point of departure is that it has scarcely ever been presented in its separate and pure form nor was its particular power yet assessed in psychoanalytic literature. I mean the impression of self-sufficiency which the love-object, man or woman, originally makes upon a member of the other sex. This factor otherwise neglected in its importance for the laws of attraction is, of course, rarely to be found in its pure form and is in general combined with other qualities of the admired object, but it is not often missed as one of the attractive trends in psychological analysis of love and of sexual desire. The impression of self-sufficiency is, in general, that the person is independent of the affection or of the aid of others and has confidence in his own strength, ability or endowment. The state or the quality of being independent is best described separately for the case of love and sex. The person who seems to be self-sufficient has the center of gravity in himself and irresistibly allures another person who is in a state of self-dislike, self-criticism or discontent with himself or herself. There is the woman who appears to be satisfied with herself, her beauty and charm and does not seem to need to be loved on account of her self-love. She entices and challenges the man to break into her self-sufficiency to induce his own discontent in her and to break the walls down between her and him. Her inner peacefulness, her reserve and her freedom from troubles, her quietness and restfulness are provoking and are tempting the man to disturb her self-sufficiency and emotional peace. The appearance of not being driven by sexual desires works as an added stimulus in the man who wants to arouse in her the same emotions which he, attracted to her, experiences. But also the woman is often impressed by the appearance of self-sufficiency in a man. It somewhere irks her that he is not more susceptible to her charm or her personality and that he is occupied with other and more important things. But are there or should there be more important things for him when she is there? The appearance of self-sufficiency is one of the strongest challenges for both sexes. Women are only more able to disguise and conceal its effects than men.

3. PARENTHOOD

The duality of parenthood is felt much more lastingly and intensively by the woman than by the man. A man looking at his child will rarely search for resemblance with the mother whereas a woman will find physical and characterological features similar to the father in her child. The emotions accompanying such perceptions are, of course, various ones according to the attitude of the woman to the child's father. Day-dreams of having a child from the beloved man are much more frequent with the woman than the corresponding fantasies with the man. They occupy the mind of the not yet pregnant woman. She will delight in anticipating a resemblance with the father in the yet-to-be baby. On the other hand, she will turn intense feelings of anger and hate, experienced against the man, against the child. A patient in the last months of pregnancy who had an attack of rage against her husband, beat the lower part of her own body with both fists. The emotional situation of the mother is also complicated by the fact that her attitude to the child is not only determined by her feelings towards his father, but by those towards herself. She will love and hate the child as representative of herself since a child is, as a patient expressed it, "part of my guts." The deep conflict between the hate against the unfaithful father and the child and her own maternal tenderness towards the child is perhaps best expressed in Medea's aria in Cherubini's opera. The clash of opposing feelings is there put into powerful music. Properly seen, Jason and the children Medea has from him are unconsciously a single entity: the children are part of him, are he, incorporated in them.

A man who becomes a father is as proud as a peacock when he distributes the cigars to his colleagues in the office. He behaves as if he had performed a miracle in producing a child while the wife's part was negligible. I heard a man discussing the problem in a drugstore in the following manner, "I ask you: when I put a dime into that Automat and a cup of chocolate comes out, whose chocolate is it, mine or the Automat's?" He appreciates his part in the process very highly. In reality the chocolate was already in the Automat and he has only given his penny's worth.

4. METAMORPHOSES

Sometimes women can accomplish the most astonishing changes in character, attitude and condition when, consciously or unconsciously, they want to get a certain man. There is, for instance, the attitude of calculated helplessness and utter dependence on others in mature women who know the world. In some cases they behave as if they were not familiar with the most ordinary things in life and need the support and advice of the man. Led to the last consequences, they simulate the behavior of a baby in order to get a baby.

There are other roles women play with a virtuosity any actor would admire. A young girl, secretary in an industrial enterprise, reports in her analytic sessions that her boss courts her and is eager to have an affair with her. While she pretends to escape his attentions, she unconsciously does everything to attract him. Yet she complains "He plays a cat-and-mouse game with me." It becomes more and more clear that the real situation is just the opposite of that presented by her. The roles are reversed; the man tries in vain to escape from her subtle kind of cornering him. Here are changes of roles surpassing not only the Metamorphoses by Ovid, but also all others transmitted to us in ancient mythologies and sagas. Where is a transformation described in which a cat is transformed into a mouse and a mouse into a cat while the two animals still think that they act as before in pursuit and flight?

5. Voices

It might be worthwhile to observe the impressions voices of the same sex make upon men and women. They are very different. It rarely happens that the voice of a man in conversation, or in lecturing, makes another man nervous or has an irritating effect. If this does occur, it is liable to be when the man's voice is high pitched or "feminine." Yet, the reaction to women's voices is, apparently, quite different. I will quote a long passage from the letter of an unknown correspondent, apparently a young woman, who had read my book *Of Love and Lust*. She writes, "If you forgive me for proceeding in true 'Autocrateness over the breakfast table' regarding your discussion of womanliness and femininity, doesn't it seem ironical that the more loquacious of the sexes has been equipped with such an inferior instrument with which to 'loquate'? A woman's voice is not a pleasant thing to hear (particularly in multiples of more than two). Shakespeare noted it when he said of some exceptional creature 'her voice was ever soft and low, a lovely thing in a woman.' Few female voices are both soft and low in their natural register. Listen to the room in which as few as three women have collected to chat (an even better listening post is a heavily womaned cocktail party) and you soon notice how exasperating, how utterly exhausting, how irritating is the high pitched conspiracy of sound they produce. Perhaps it is this harsh detergent effect upon the nerves of which men really speak when they complain about their wives' incessant nagging. Not her words, rather the sound of her words in motion—there's the rub. I noticed this unconsciously several years ago when I attended a girls' school entirely staffed by women. Since then, I've heard several men and women complain of their difficulties in tolerating the best of women teachers. I'm inclined to believe that what they found so difficult to tolerate, at least in part, was not the woman's teaching techniques, but the wearing effects of her voice. A woman's voice gets on her own nerves at times, though she is usually unconscious of the fact that that is the origin of her tension, and would be in any case reluctant to admit it. But a man's voice, with its finely honed edges, is that of the king: lions, tigers and bears command his every word as though his voice were yet another God-given symbol of virility, one more safeguard of his potency, another factor reassuring his status as the first sex. What a pleasant sound a roomful of men make—hearty, confident—a sound that the nerves could withstand indefinitely. A man might be a fool, but he has a far greater chance of commanding an audience than a woman with four college degrees. Whereas woman, poor penisless creature, paltry second-best sex that she is, is sentenced to bleat and to harp, screech and whine, or tinkle her silly silver bells for the rest of her days. It is as if, under the falsetto to which she has been consigned, one may always detect traces of latent hysteria, a note of uncertainty that eventually will dash all her pretentious notions to fluff. (I additionally suspect that when a woman writer is pilloried, when her words are dismissed as 'typically feminine,' and 'obviously the work of a woman,' that it is the memory of the inferiority of the female voice unconsciously ringing in the critic's ear.) That melodious quality which Shakespeare found so captivating, is indeed a rarity. Silver tongues are as scarce as partridge tongues. It might be interesting to add that women are best-loved when they have learned the art of good listening."

One need not agree on all points with the views of the unknown writer of this letter to find it very perceptive and amusing. It is at all events interesting to hear a woman speak with candor about men's and women's voices although one will assume that she is not free from bias. But are any of us?

6. LOOKING AT THE OTHER MAN, THE OTHER WOMAN

Here is one fragment of dialogue contrasted with another one: A woman asks her husband, "Who was that man?" The husband, "Which man?" "The one who just passed. You looked at him. Do you know him?" "No, I know *of* him. He is the vice-president of the publicity firm with which we have some dealings."

A husband asks his wife, "Who was that woman?" The wife, "You mean the one who just passed? I don't know her." "You looked at her so attentively. Why?" "Well, she wore just the kind of hat I wanted to buy. They sell them at that shop on Madison Avenue and 72nd Street." "You looked at her so long, I thought you knew her." "No, I wanted to see what accessories she wore with it and what sort of dress she wore."

In the contrast between these dialogue-fragments more is reflected than the difference between the ways a man and a woman look at an unknown person of the same sex who might pass by them in a restaurant or on the street. Generally men do not pay much attention to other men upon these occasions. Women, though, do. Their motives seem generally to be curiosity and interest of different kinds ("What does she wear?"), vaguely psychological ("What kind of woman is she?"), and generally human ("What kind of a person is she?"). The two first kinds of interest are usually absent or little

developed in man looking at other men. Even when one of
them exists it is liable to be restricted to a narrow realm such
as the profession or the achievements of the other man. In
women the range of interest runs the gamut from hat to shoes,
from attractive features of the personality to unpleasant ones
even from personal relationship to oneself to possibilities of
relations with the other sex.

7. SELF-DISLIKE

The phenomenon of self-dislike or self-hate is only apparently a solitary one. In psychological reality two people are
present in self-dislike: the self sees and examines itself with
the eyes of others, originally of the mother and the father,
to which later on other loved or respected persons are added.
Self-like is the unconscious continuation of the early delight
mother had in her baby and self-dislike reflects the imagined
distaste or aversion mother would feel in herself. It is not
accidental that self-dislike starts regularly at one's own body
and then goes over to one's mental or moral attributes since
the baby was first seen only as a body. The grown-up man
disliking himself can thus imagine how his mother looked at
him with violent distaste when he was born. From the depth
of his despair the biblical Job opened his mouth and cursed
the day of his birth, "Let the day perish wherein I was born,
and the night in which it was said, 'There is a man child
conceived.' " Hate for one's own moral self is already a displacement of this original form of looking at oneself and
often remains intimately connected with seeing one's own
countenance. Oscar Wilde's *The Picture of Dorian Gray* confirms this concept of the psychological nature of self-dislike.

8. The Coming Morality

To get along with oneself is one of the first conditions of social life. Only a person who gets along with himself or who can tolerably live with himself will be able to live with others without too great emotional disturbances. The first and most important commandment of our coming ethics is, "Love yourself more than your neighbor," otherwise you will hate your neighbor. There are many persons so dissatisfied with themselves—men more frequently than women—that you can say that they go through life being cross with themselves.

Others are not even on speaking terms with themselves and thus prevent an improvement in the relationship with themselves and others. In such cases of self-hate the demand "Love thy neighbor as thyself" amounts to misanthropic advice. Poor neighbor! A Jewish proverb says, "He who is not good to himself cannot be good to others."

Hostility against onself leads, often in the form of unconscious projection, to most disastrous consequences, even to war. A modern Polonius would advise his son:

> "This above all: to thine own self be good,
> And it must follow, as the night the day,
> Thou canst not then be bad to any man."

Women more often than men console themselves and decide: "I'll be good to myself if no one else is." It is in such a mood that they often go out and buy themselves a new dress or a new hat. Men are more belligerent than women and have difficulties in living with themselves in peace.

9. PAST LOVE

A man who is jilted by a woman will generally overcome the experience in a shorter time than a woman in a similar situation. This is particularly true if the relationship had been a sexual one and of not too long duration. Here are two cases from psychoanalytic practice for comparison. A man had an affair with a much younger girl whom he could not marry. It lasted for two years. Then the young girl found someone else whom she decided to marry. The man felt hurt but conquered the desire for the woman and consoled himself with another girl. He had almost forgotten his previous sweetheart when he met her with her husband at a party. He behaved very naturally towards both and did not experience any intense emotions.

Another case: a young girl had had a sexual affair of several months with an older man. She recognized that her lover was tired of her. Deeply hurt, she withdrew. After some time, she became infatuated with another man, but the memory of her previous lover was still alive. Seeing him again at a party she behaved aloof toward him, but still felt hurt and found some satisfaction in the thought that she had been very well dressed and that her present lover was a representative social figure who showed in his behavior at the party that he cared for her.

Neglecting for the moment the individual differences of the two cases, I am inclined to assume that they present some features of typical masculine and feminine behavior patterns and of the emotional attitudes of the sexes. Assuming that similar circumstances are present, we would conclude that two main reasons determine the divergencies. The disappointment of the woman has a deeper and more lasting effect because a sexual relationship for her is rarely restricted to the realm of sensual satisfaction. In general, an emotional involvement preceeds or results from this kind of relationship, but not necessarily so for the man. Furthermore the disappointment hurts the woman much more because it affects her pride and ego feelings more deeply than those of the man in a similar situation. Finally, but not least, a woman who enters a sexual relationship often hopes (sometimes against hope) that it will culminate in marriage, a presupposition which is lacking in the man.

10. ASCETICISM AND THE SUPER-EGO

A patient had subjected himself to a very rigid self-discipline. He always dressed completely after leaving his bath and never allowed himself any small comforts like house-shoes and so on. Once when he had an extraordinary success in his profession he, coming home, permitted himself to take off his jacket, to lie down on the couch and to have a glass of whisky. In telling me about this relaxation he tried to justify it by saying, "I gave myself those comforts as one gives a beggar some money."

There are certain processes and emotional developments in the one sex which the other does not understand or understands to a very limited extent because their physiological and biological premises are missing. Which man really (not only intellectually) knows what goes on in a woman before menstruation sets in? Which mother comprehends the urgency of sexual drives in her son during puberty? Can she emotionally imagine his desperate fight against masturbation, his vows not to yield to the temptation and his unavoidable relapses? Women do not easily recognize even the conflict some ascetic men have with their strong sexual drives. I had a patient who whenever he felt sexually very excited jumped from his bed into an ice-cold shower, to avoid masturbation. Women in general are not violently tempted by sexual desires, but they would not go to such lengths of fighting them nor undertake such desperate measures of defense against them.

The rigidity and severity of conscience reaches its peak in certain male cases of compulsion and obsession. It is as if the patients who often dissimulate their disturbance were perpetually under the order of an iron and unrelenting discipline. Their behavior reminds one of that of an Austrian sergeant who told his recruits: "Look here, I am a kind fellow, but when I am in the service I am a beast and I am always in the service."

Boys have frequent dreams of glory: they often see themselves then as supermen. Girls have less frequent dreams of glory and they see themselves in them sometimes as men.

Little girls are less resistant to washing and combing and other chores than little boys. I heard in Vienna that a little boy looked on as his grandmother dusted the furniture and later on asked her. "Why have I always to be washed? Could you not dust me as you did the pictures?"

Psychoanalysts agree that the super-ego development in men and women is different, that the super-ego of the average man is severer in its demands and stricter in its punishments than that of the woman. The difference is certainly to a great extent determined by the fact that the super-ego reacts to aggressiveness within the individual. The hostile and aggressive drives of the male are more intense than those of the female—at least, of the human kind, while the female of many animal species is supposed to be more ferocious, more deadly than the male.

One gets a good idea of the formation of the super-ego in men when one considers its early phases within the boy, especially the period in which the transition from fear of punishment to inner demands takes place. Here are two instances of this initial state: a little boy was sent by his mother to the Chinese laundry where he was to deliver some bundles. The boy did this and the laundry-man confirmed the receipt of the package on a little piece of paper. On the way home the child lost this note and was terror-stricken. He did not dare to go home and wandered through the streets imagining that his misdeed would bring ruin to his whole family. Many hours later the police picked the child up and brought him home where the parents were panicky.

The other example: a boy in elementary school had developed a shyly concealed infatuation for a little girl in his own class. Dark sexual desires were clearly fused with his admiration. He wrote on a little paper a few four-letter words which in his imagination expressed his love-feeling and threw the paper from his bench to his amorata. The teacher saw this and intercepted the note which he read. He told the boy that he had to stay behind in class while the other children could leave. The little boy was apprehensive and afraid, but when he was finally left alone with the teacher, the teacher told him to wipe the blackboard clean, to distribute books and gave him other tasks otherwise alloted to privileged pupils. The patient had kept the name of this teacher in his memory. When he came to me, he was a man of forty-two years. His voice still broke when he told me of this experience.

PART SIX

Sexuality of The Sexes

1. IMAGERY IN SEX

Marriage with a frigid wife or with a weakly potent husband favors the emergence of sexual images—especially of those founded on memories—of very satisfying sexual intercourse. In those memories the man will remember the words, gestures and movements in which a woman responded to his love-making while a woman will rather imagine the corresponding words, gestures and movements of her male partner, making love to her. She will get excited by the memory of how ardently he desired her while the man will get sexually aroused by the memory of the passionate and lusty response which his desire awakened in the woman. The selectivity of memory will in the case of those recollections be determined not only by one's own desire, but be helped by the recalling of the sensual urge of one's partner.

It is, however, significant how the imagery of women and men in general differ. The fantasies of women usually start with memories of how the man admired and wooed them. There are phantasies of his approach in the form of caresses and sweet words. These phantasies only slowly pass over to sexual images. The phantasies of men go much more directly and immediately to the remembered sexual scenes. When a woman's imagery regularly begins immediately with sexual

pictures without preceding affectionate or tender prelimi-
naries, one can with great likelihood assume strong masculine
components. When on the other hand a man in his sexual
fantasies dwells a long time on scenes of affection and pro-
longs in his imagination the prelude too much, one might
conclude that there is a great part of femininity in his personality.

2. THE SEXUAL LIFE OF THE TWO SEXES

The curiosity of women is directed to finding out personal
things about people, the curiosity of men more to discoveries
of the hidden and concealed sides of nature. Personal relations don't interest men as much as they do women. When
men are more drawn to the discovery of the world's secret,
it is, as if the finding of the concealed female genitals had a
prototypical significance for the character of man's curiosity.

The mystery which woman has for men has its origin in
the secret location of their genital organs. The intensive
desire to find out their nature, so strong in little boys, is in
psychological reality never entirely satisfied. The mystery
remains although male children discover that the female
genitals are different from theirs. Although their exploration
was at least partly successful, the secrecy is for the boy, so to
speak, perpetuated. It is as if the result of the inquiry were
only superficially acknowledged while it was on the deeper
level rejected or denied.

On account of this reaction the man unconsciously expects
some extraordinary discovery every time he is to see a woman
undressed although he is consciously well aware that he will
find in the one woman the same as in the other ("Cover her
face with the Stars and Stripes and it's all the same"). Here

is thus a simultaneous ignorance and knowledge that prepares man for what he will find and makes him nevertheless look forward to it as if to the discovery of something new. This goes so far that even gynecologists are developing a curiosity for what they may expect whenever they conquer a new woman. It is not remarkable that they too experience sexual desire or appetite—also cooks must eat—but their curiosity remains alive although they know best what they will find. It is as if the cooks expect surprises from dishes whose recipe is well known to them.

In the fantasies of men and women even more than in their actions it becomes obvious that consciously or unconsciously sexual arousal is connected with two persons. It needs two not only to quarrel, but also to get sexually excited. In the fantasies the sexual object often appears alone, but the person who desires her is unconsciously there or is to be supplemented. In the absence of the sexual object its role is taken over by the day-dreamer himself or herself who plays both parts as some actors can play a woman and her lover if no other actor is present.

In the sexual arousal of the man there is a certain point at which each delay results in decrease of intensity or in defective performance. The difference in the time of arousal in man and woman makes it necessary that the man postpones his orgasm out of consideration for his sexual partner. When, however, a point of no return is reached, the man has to go ahead without thought of the woman, without regard for her and without waiting for her. Only in this way will he reach his gretest pleasure, but will he also secure the best sexual gratification for his mate. In being "selfish" in this enlightened sense, he will be altruistic, while being too "considerate" and thoughtful of his partner leads to self-privation and spoiling of sexual enjoyment for her. That moment in which the animal, selfish nature of male sexuality breaks through and legitimately brushes all other considerations aside is subjectively clearly experienced and is not uncertain. It is prescribed by the rhythm of the male excitement and timed with the precision of a metronome. It amounts to a signal "Now or never."

Freud, as we have said, asserted that sexuality in its essential character is masculine also when appearing in a woman. This is perhaps no problem for the psychologist, but for biologists. There is, however, a kind of indirect proof for Freud's theory in a fact rarely, if ever mentioned in the books on sex, namely the induction of sexual arousal and activity of the woman by the man. A man who had much experiences in his sexual life asserted that long continued gentle stroking of the nipples awakens in most women the wish to grasp the penis and stroke it as if this were the appropriate and corresponding reaction. He asserted that here is a field for scientific experiment, namely an attempt at answer to the question: how long can a woman remain passive when she is caressed in the described manner before she feels the tendency to react in that form of active response.

Most men indulge in kissing and other caresses only before sexual intercourse. Most women wish in vain their mates would also kiss them and caress them "outside the bedroom" and without the intention of going to bed immediately.

There are significant fantasies of female masochists in which no degradation nor sexual misuse is central, but rejection of the woman as a desirable sexual object—in contrast to the fantasies of male masochists. Here is a typical fantasy of a middle-aged woman whose day-dreams take frequently a novel-like form: In one of the scenes she imagines a Shah of Persia who plays chess with his vizier. During the game an eunuch presents to the king many women who want to become members of the emperor's harem. One woman after the other appears entirely nude for the presentation, among them the daydreamer. When she steps forward and, as ordered, silently turns around so that her full nude figure is seen, the Shah looks up from the chessboard, makes a gesture meaning no and says to the vizier "Your move!" as if he had disliked the interruption of the game. Here is another fantasy of the same woman: in a town in Austria an army division arrives for maneuvers. The general and his adjutant leave the mess-hall after dinner. The patient waits for them near the exit, makes a curtsy and says "Good evening! Please I am the town-whore." Fantasies of this kind aroused the patient sexually. They would have not the same effect on a man.

Promiscuity of men cannot be used in their masochistic fantasies while promiscuity of woman is in our Western civilization conceived as degrading. One cannot say of a man who is sexually promiscuous that he makes himself "cheap."

There are agent provocateurs not only in politics and in the cold war of the world-powers, but also in the private or semi-private area of sexuality. There are women and men who are not "teasers" in the usual sense nor is their aim as simple as to lead on persons of the other sex. Nor is their behavior dictated by the wish to convince themselves of their power to attract the partner, but rather by the anticipated enjoyment of his or her frustration. A young woman was very aware of this and only a reactive pity for her "victim" prevented her from doing the last steps. A young man who wooed her with great passion was—she guessed—latently homosexual and impotent with women. She tried to seduce him whereby she looked forward to his sexual failure with some cruel satisfaction. The thought that held her finally back, was expressed in the sentence: "The poor boy! He would faint, if I would suddenly say yes to his proposition-ing me." Such provocation is also well known in homosexual circles, for instance a man tries to attract another man by all methods in order to act very astonished when the other, thus provoked, takes the sexual initiative. The agent provocateur protests then violently and is astonished; he indignantly denies that he is homosexually oriented: "Who me?"

It should not be denied that the sexual urge of the male has an aggressive and even a sadistic character and the wish to intrude the female body amounts to a kind of forceful incursion. The drive is not restricted to the drainage of secretion. The opening and invasion of another territory belongs to the realm of forepleasure comparable to that of forcing a door. The gradual extension and yielding of the female genitals enhances the enjoyment. It is diminished by the absence of certain physical sensations developed during the action. A patient complained that the "entrance" into his wife's body was "too easy." He said that she is "as wide as a barn."

Freud pointed out to us that one of the first manifestations of the sexual drive in adolescent boys is a wish to throw stones in windows and similar symptoms. Even the sexual curiosity of small boys has this aggressive, intrusive character. The analyst will frequently hear of childhood memories in which the little boy lying on the ground tried to look up the skirts of relatives or maids and was reproached for such indecent curiosity. Peeping tendencies amount to a desire to take possession of the object by means of seeing it. Voyeuristic tendencies have always this sadistic undertone that pervades even the artistic production of painters and photographers.

It is not accidental that the language of the photographers speaks of "shooting a picture."

The seeming exception from the predominence of aggressiveness in male sexuality is shown by examples in which the male wants the woman to take the sexual initiative. In most of these cases the man tentatively plays, so to speak, the role of the passive woman and vicariously experiences her forms of enjoyment.

Men much oftener than women feel the urge to experience sexual pleasure as such, without regard to the object, "sex in the raw," as a patient called it. This particular pleasure is tied to the condition of seeing in the woman only the sexual object, a female, spreading her thighs apart and surrendering to man's lust. A patient who was, so to speak, of a capricious potency could have satisfactory sexual intercourse with his wife only when he, before approaching her, verbally degraded her using many four-letter words for sexual actions, telling her that she wanted to feel him inside her and so on. His attitude was not only an attempt to degrade or humiliate his wife but to lower her imaginary elevated position, to make her accessible as a sexual object. It was necessary to bring her down from the elevated stand at which he saw her in order to put himself near her on the level of a sexually accessible object. Other forms of sexual gratification in which he did not describe verbal degradation, called "sex-washing" by him—an expression analogous to brain-washing—was not as satisfactory because he missed that prelude in which his craving for "pure sex" appeared.

The new-born baby is put into the crib and kept warm and cozy. Light and noise are avoided near him. The transition from life within the womb to a new independent existence is facilitated by a kind of artificial restoration of life in mother's womb, by a situation, as close to its previous form of existence as possible. In sexual intercourse the woman becomes soft and pliant and adjusts her own body to that of the man, fits it into place with his until the bodies are locked as far as possible for grown-ups to be together. The female body surrounds the male as the cradle once did the baby and moistens the man's body penetrating her. A Swiss proverb, several times quoted by Freud, says, "Love is homesickness." The proverb is not meant as a definition of the sexual urge, but rather as a characterization of its nature: at least as it is experienced by the man, namely as search for home. But this presupposes that home is not only a place where one unpacks, but also where the aim of all wishes is situated. From this characterization it can be concluded that it is not a place of which one is afraid nor of which one thinks with boredom. It cannot be imagined as a place of unrest or conflict, but as one at which peace is found. Not only comfort, but also redemption. In this sense sexual satisfaction in a mature sense is comparable to an oasis desired on the march through the desert. But such an oasis is rare and the visions of man's excited fantasy often prove that they are not miracles, but mirages.

If a woman were in her right mind she should be sometimes able to have an affair without getting emotionally involved. But when is a woman in her right mind? And would a woman be able to remain emotionally uninvolved in an affair and remain a woman except in an anatomical sense?

Men don't realize how smug they become after they have been living with a woman for a long time. They don't know that no woman likes to be taken for granted and each wishes always to be wooed anew. She would rather be pursued and

caught and held again than to be left restful and content in
her cage where her mate can find her whenever he wishes to.

The concept that girls are all sugar and spice in contrast
with the properties of boys can lead to disastrous emotional
consequences when the boys grow up. It can result in shyness
and impotence as well as in an unconscious tendency to
humiliate and degrade women, to tear them down and pull
them into the gutter. The astonishing outcome of this immature view is that its unconscious continuation can result
in those two opposite attitudes towards women.

It is well known among psychiatrists and psychologists
that fetishism as sexual perversion or attitude is very rare
with women, compared with its frequency among men. This
is the more astonishing since women are inclined to per-
sonalize inanimate objects and have basically an animistic
Weltbild. Yet they do not worship parts of man's cloth,
neither his shoes nor his stockings nor other objects belonging to him, separated from his body. Objects of the man as
such do not play a very important role in woman's sexual
fantasies. Yet women highly appreciate gifts men have given
them and attribute a highly sentimental value to them; the
highest, of course, to them is the ring on their finger. The
high estimation of this symbolic object does not transcend
its area and certainly does not arouse sexual desire for the
man. The fact that fetishism is much rarer in women than
in men, is an indirect confirmation for Freud's thesis that a
fetish has the substitute function of a sexualized part of the
woman's body.

A man sitting down may be careful or careless with regard
to his pants and a woman with regard to her skirts. In the
case of the woman there is a third possibility—she may be
purposely careless.

An American woman who knew that her husband had a mistress in the years in which he was overseas during the Second World War took this affair for granted, but when she found out that he had a child with the woman in England she became deeply disturbed. She dreamed every night that the other woman swam with the child on her breasts through the ocean to land in America and she awakened always with anxiety. A wife was told that her husband kept company with a younger woman: a lady friend asked the wife whether she believed that the husband was having an affair with that woman or only social companionship. She answered with the counterquestion, "He is a man, isn't he?" The jealousy of women is not restricted to the sexual field. A wife would mind it very much if another woman were to suggest that she should mend her husband's socks or sew on a button on his suit—even if she were convinced that there were no sexual relations between the husband and the other woman.

A patient follows his thought-associations: I played squash yesterday at the club. It was not a question if I would win or lose. Important was that I played without conviction. I really did not give a damn. . . What comes to mind is a cross-section . . . namely that's the way I have sex-intercourse with my wife. In my married life I feel hemmed in, fenced in as in a concentration-camp. I go home from the office and then it is like a blank, a tabula rasa. . . . You know they have excavated ancient Assyrian tablets with many curses on them and the last of the curses is: "May nothing new happen to thou." That is the mood I feel in when I go home and think of sexual intercourse.

I asserted fifteen years ago in my book *Psychology of Sex-*

*Relations** that there is no such thing as one-sided satisfaction in sexual intercourse. I have found since much evidence proving that I was mistaken and I am using this opportunity to correct my error. First of all I have to point out that the validity of that statement is in the majority of the cases restricted to the genital region of the couple in sexual intercourse. Even there, there are exceptions, for instance the case of the sadist or the raper, who experiences sexual satisfaction. Also in the area of other sexual perversions one-sided gratification occurs quite frequently. There is, furthermore not only sexual satisfactions in sexual intercourse. The process can fulfill ego-needs and give satisfaction of a non-sexual kind, for instance gratify a woman's wish to be desired by a man or her need to give him emotional and sexual release. It is, of course, much more frequent that selffish, one-sided sexual pleasure especially of a sadistic kind if enjoyed by the man. There are, however, exceptional cases in which the woman is satisfied while the man remains unsatisfied. It is psychologically interesting what emotional reactions are then experienced by the woman. In one case the husband had a sexual disturbance which concerned only the emission while his erection was maintained. (It was very likely that he unconsciously was withholding the emission.) His wife once had multiple orgasm during intercourse with him under these circumstances. It was significant that she afterwards felt guilty towards him as if she had an unfair advantage over him. She called her attitude—very characteristically—"unfeminine." She had the vague feeling that it is imperative that the wife should give gratification to the husband while for her sexual satisfaction is less important. Another time she said she felt like a "whore" on account of her one-sided enjoyment.

* Farrar & Rinehart, New York, 1945.

Love-making is to most women a sacred activity following its own rhythm and cannot be interrupted without serious damage. If there is a pause, the sacred service has to be started anew, exactly as the rites of ancient religions. Any interruption is experienced as unpleasant. Women say: "Don't stop kissing me."

When women take the initiative in the relationship with men and are pursuing instead of waiting to be pursued, it is not always due to the lack of energy on the side of the male. Women sometimes feel that they are not attractive or desirable enough and therefore have to take the sexual initiative. In other words: they have not developed enough self-confidence and self-assurance to be able to wait. They don't trust their charm enough and cannot afford to take the feminine role. It is thus anxiety that drives them from passivity into a kind of provoking activity.

The contrasting feminine and masculine attitude to the male genitals are reflected in the dreams of two patients who approached the end of their psychoanalytic treatment. The woman who had to conquer intensive feelings of hostility against men and who had sometimes the impulse to tear her husband's penis off dreamed, "I have a baby and I feel very motherly to it, stroke and caress it. It is a tiny baby, but it grows rapidly and becomes very big." In the interpretation of the dream the baby and the penis form an unconscious unit. The motherly feeling and affection of the childless woman for the genitals of her husband marks the transition to the acceptance of her femininity. A man who had not been sexually potent and had been burdened with many doubts about his virility dreamed, "I am promoted to organization man." The thought-associations of the patient circled around the recent book, *"The Organization Man,"* which in the thoughts of the patient means a raised rank or condition. The keyword of the latent dream-content is revealed in the pun "Organ" which concerns, of course, the male organ. The motherly feeling of the woman towards the penis and the man's pride in his organ are symptomatic for both patients' progress and their readiness to take the appropriate sex-role.

The community of bed and table is appropriate also for the comparison of a couple's sex life. Many men behave like ungallant husbands also in their sexual life: while the wife is still busy setting the table they already begin to eat. While the wife begins to nibble at the food, the husband is already in the middle of his meal. He has satisfied his hunger and is ready to leave the table while she just begins to enjoy the food, *"l'appétit vient en mangeant."* He is perhaps already a little disgusted with her appetite since he is already sated.

A patient tried in the evening before his analytic session to remember and to count all women with whom he slept during his forty-five years. He told me that he counted fifty-three and was very proud of this number. The number is not important, but rather the fact that he had not been emotionally involved with any of these women, that none of them meant much to him. To continue this train of thought: Don Juan possessed an incredible number of mistresses, but what was their significance for his emotional life? You remember Leporello's aria ("But in Spain thousand and three"). Seen from a higher point of view, the list does not belong to the area of a man's love-life, but to that of statistics.

The guiltfeelings due to adultery can always be traced back to incestuous desires because they were at first directed to a forbidden object and towards forbidden sexual relation. These desires have thus a pattern-forming significance. The special stimulus of guiltfeeling connected with illegitimate relations has its roots in those primal incestuous wishes. One would expect that most men would feel less guiltfeeling about forbidden sexuality than women, but this is not so. Women feel those relations as improper and are afraid of a bad social reputation. But men feel more guilty in connection with sexuality because their sex-drives are connected with their much more intensive aggressiveness. Men have to grapple with the problem of an invisible enemy who condemns and forbids their lawless sexual wishes. The prototype of this interfering person is, of course, the father whom they have to remove (unconsciously kill) to reach the desired object. The sexual guiltfeelings of the woman will be weaker, the moral demands of woman are less intensive and urgent.

When a woman fears losing a man she loves she abandons herself often to him sexually, hoping thus to keep him with her. As everybody knows, this hope is frequently frustrated. The man whose sexual appetite for her is satisfied is for this reason not tied any longer to the woman. On the other hand the woman feels herself tied by a deeper and more lasting bond because of the common sexual experiences. The situation reminds one of a similar position in war in which a person goes out to conquer an enemy and succeeds to make him prisoner—but in doing so is captured himself. Men sometimes try to overcome the resistances of a woman by pretending to love her. Women sometimes use the lure of sex in the hope that man will begin to love them.

A man gave a woman a ring with the inscription *"Plus qu'hier, moins que demain"* (More than yesterday, less than tomorrow), obviously to describe his love for her. The inscription would in general be more appropriate to characterize the kind of love a woman feels for the man than the other way. There is more to woman's love than meets the eye glancing at such a ring. A woman once said to a man: "The more I do for you, cooking, washing and ironing the more you belong to me." This is not only possessive, but also motherly. Men have no similar feelings.

Freud thought that the sexual drives emerge first in conjunction with the self-preserving drives and that their primal object is the mother who feeds the child and takes care of it. It is very likely that also the origin of that sublime experience called love has to be searched for in the same area and manifests itself in the primal form of expected gratification of hunger and thirst. More than sixty years ago a Viennese newspaper published a contest for its women readers, asking them to answer the question: "What is the best way to keep a man's love?" The prize was given to the lapidar answer: "Feed the beast well!"

Sexual memories of the man circle all around the sexual behavior of his partners, of their surrender and the intensity of their response. The sexual memories of the woman revive images of the man's intensity of wooing and of his desire for her.

Freud pointed out that the things we hold highest in our esteem are by subterranean ties connected with the objects we abhor and by which we are repelled. In contrast with the idealization of woman by man, women themselves have not developed a similar kind of adoration for the man. But neither do they experience a tendency to degrade the sexual object comparable to the secret trends of many men. They do not put man on a pedestal but neither do they feel the emotional need to tear him into the dust.

Much of the confusion in scientific discussions on sexual questions is due to the fact that we do not differentiate enough longing for affection and sexual desire. The French distinguish the *"besoin de tendresse"* and the *"besoin de volupté."* The first is stronger in women and with them, in general preceeds the second. The *"besoin de volupté"* is stronger in men and overshadows in its importance the first craving.

After sexual intercourse, women often feel the wish that their partner should express his love or tenderness for them. A woman sometimes expressed this wish directly saying: "Say something loving to me" to the man who was silent. Such a need is very rarely experienced by the man after sexual intercourse. It is as though for him all was said and done in the sexual act.

The fact that women never stop going to beauty-salons proves that they are blessed with a superb optimism. Also the efforts to increase their desirability by make-up obeys, the older they get, the law of diminishing returns.

The case of a number of men who replace frustrated sexual desire by oral satisfaction in over-eating confirms Freud's theory that the sexual appetite had originally an oral character. The regression to this primal phase has also the effect that sexual desire seems to diminish as if it gives its place to its predecessor. People say, "A good cock does not get fat."

Sometimes men feel they have to have sexual intercourse for hygienic reasons, just as they have to eat three meals daily because it is necessary from the point of health. They indulge then in sex without great desire, so to speak without appetite. Viewing sexual activity from the point of view of health is generally alien to women. Yet I heard a woman after not too satisfactory sexual intercourse say: "Well, perhaps it was good for my complexion."

A young man conceives of his compulsive masturbation as a compromise of sexual gratification and punishment for that

forbidden activity. He advanced the theory that the colloquialism "to jerk oneself off" proves that masturbation has
also the character of self-castration. The same patient sometimes regretted the vain abundance of unproductive sperma-
tozoa of young men and imagined that in this way millions
of lives were lost to mankind. Masturbation was for him the
"wasteland of sexuality."

A woman who during sexual intercourse plans the menu
for tomorrow and considers if she should cook carrots or
beans can still be usable as a sexual object. A man who during the same process begins to ponder the pros and cons of
a business-transaction will become shortly impotent.

Sexual desire and hostility exclude each other. The one
has to yield its place before the other can prevail. This is not
so with cruelty because the fusion of sexual urge and cruelty
is possible and is known under the name of sadism. Sadistic
tendencies in general are not identical with hostility. There
is even a strange kind of attraction to the victim of sadism.

It is not difficult for a woman to leave a man she does not
love any more. It is much more difficult for her to leave him
as long as she feels he still loves her.

An often overlooked condition necessary to overcome the
emotional resistances to free expressions of sexual desire and
fulfillment in woman is that the man in arousal and performance is unselfconscious and uninhibited. Even a trace of
inhibition in him makes her self-conscious and becomes an
obstacle in sexual expression while his being uninhibited
frees her from her own inhibitions. A woman, married to a
man of typical New England mentality to whom sexual
processes at that time appeared as somewhere shameful or
sinful, went to bed with her husband as often as he demanded, but remained frigid with him because his clumsy

and inhibited sexual behavior blocked her in the development of her sexuality. The well-educated and refined woman had periodical sexual adventures with men of a much lower social and cultural level. She let herself be picked up by those men whom she despised but with whom she reached sexual orgasm. In her psychoanalytic sessions she stated that her husband's attitude made her feel self-conscious and ashamed of her sexuality.

All young women sometimes feel the fear that by making love to a man they may appear unlovely to him.

Men are freed by the fulfillment of sexual desire, women are committed by it. The same act often means release for the one sex and bondage for the other.

A patient remembered an attractive young girl whose acquaintance he made at a party and with whom he had a long and interesting conversation. They sat together in the corner of a room. The host taking care of his guests came over and asked them if he should give them something to drink. The man remembered the answer of the girl with pleasure after several years, "No, thank you. We don't need any liquor," she said, "we have each other." The man felt as if she had drawn a magic circle around them both with those words.

Pascal's phrase that the self is hateful ("Le moi est haissable") will not be acknowledged by woman except when she looks badly. It has no moral connotation.

The melancholic recognition of the aging woman that she is not desired any longer has scarcely any analogy in the emotional life of the old man. Aging men come closest to this kind of experience when it dawns on them that they are not any longer needed in their professional life.

Women in contrast with men store compliments and endearing things said to them as squirrels keep nuts to eschew them later. When they are alone, women sometimes bring sweet things they were told out from the hiding-places of their memory and enjoy them. They have not only momentary, but also delayed pleasant reactions.

A man especially when he is young and shy might anticipate the scene in which he will declare his love to a young woman. He will perhaps imagine how surprised she will be when he proposes to her. How he is mistaken! It is never a surprise to her. She has foreseen the scene and anticipated it many times before he ever thought it could occur. He might think it is an improvisation of his while she knows that she is its stage-manager behind the wings. She had experienced many rehearsals of the play in her imagination, even dress-rehearsals.

A woman said quite astonished to her friend: "You know, men have problems too." She meant, of course, not problems connected with professional difficulties and financial worries, but emotional problems in relationships with the other sex. The fact that women are so much more emotionally dependent on men and that the greatest part of their emotional interests is concentrated on the attitude of a man, often makes them think that men have it easy in this direction and are free from emotional difficulties of a similar kind. This idea makes many women develop a wrong perspective on man.

The maturing process of the woman is more dramatic than that of the man and its decisive changes are marked by traumatic experiences whose place of actions is her body: menstruation, deflowering and childbirth, all characterized by pain and blood. The new life which woman brings into the world and the preparation for it are initiated by catastrophes within her similar to those of Earth that is subjected to vibration and quakes and inundations.

Beer-Hofmann's president in the play *Der Graf von Charolais* says a few lines expressing woman's fate:

> Not yet freed
> From those primal and mysterious contacts
> Subject still to the same nocturnal planet
> Which commands the sea, she is with every full moon
> Reminded by blood and pain, like a tardy priestess
> Of her task here below.

In sexuality woman is the person who prescribes the measure and rhythm. The man is in most cases too quick in playing the music and the woman would like, if she could but dare, to order "Andante please!" Occasionally the man is too slow and it is then even more difficult for her to accelerate the tempo because she is afraid it would appear unfeminine.

Like the conductor she is restricted to gestures, to a sign-language while the man, like some unattentive instrumentalist of an orchestra, does not pay enough attention to the conductor. The best enjoyment in sexual intercourse results, of course, when the musician is tuned in to the conductor—in this case to the woman—who leads the orchestra, but who is also considering his own individuality.

Freud taught us that the passive aim of a drive can be pursued with the greatest energy. It is not essential that this aim is consciously perceived. The singleness of the unconscious purpose can, for instance, be clearly seen in the behavior of some children who vex and test the patience of their mother so long until she loses control and scolds or punishes them. There are masochistic men who provoke their partner until she gives them the desired punishment or bestows the humiliation and degradation unconsciously wished for. In attaining this passive aim sexual perverts often develop an astonishing intensity of energy. Indefatigable and inexhaustible energy is sometimes also devoted to passive aims in the region of normal sexual life in which no pathological nor perverted satisfaction is sought. Women sometimes concentrate untiring and almost heroic efforts on the task of being seduced by a certain man.

In the homosexual relations of men jealousy and other intensive emotions sometimes lead to very violent scenes, even to murder. There is no comparable degree of violence in Lesbian relations. Even under the influence of intense emotions the conflict rarely, if ever, transgresses the bounds of punches and hair-pulling. Murder is a rare event in the conflicts of homosexual women.

The first impression one gets of a young woman entering a room, full of people, is that of concealed or well disguised insecurity. Only a few self-conscious young men have a similar attitude. It seems that the awareness of being the possessor of a penis protects man against such over self-awareness.

Woman's pride often has a function similar to the garment which the French call *"cache-misère."* It covers, conceals and protects the poor or pitiful inside.

3.   Ubiquity of Sexual Symbolism

Few psychoanalytic statements have aroused as much opposition and astonishment as Freud's theory that our dreams show a pervasing sexual symbolism in which the male and female genitals are presented as different objects of a non-sexual nature. The following paragraphs contain examples from language, literature and folklore in which the same symbols appear. All examples are such that the findings of psychoanalysis could not have influenced their character.

In his *Introductory Lecture on Psychoanalysis*, Freud re·minds the reader that a cloak, in a woman's dream is frequently a symbol for a man. He continues, "I hope you will be impressed when you hear that Reik [1920] tells us: 'In the ancient marriage ceremony of the Bedouins, the bridegroom covers the bride with a social cloak which is called "ababa" and at the same time utters the ritual words: "Let no man in the future cover thee but me.' " In the forty years since I found this confirmation of a dream symbol in ritual and folklore many psychoanalysts have recognized the same symbol in poetry, religious ceremonials and so on, but it came as a great surprise to me to find it again, and in an unveiled form in a biographical film. Last year in Vienna I saw an Austrian film which presented the life story of the popular operetta composer Emmerich Kalman (*Countess Maritza, Gypsy Princess, Sari* and so on) on the screen. I remembered that as a young man I had met the composer. I had attended the performance of some of his operettas and had enjoyed their tuneful melodies. The movie depicts the young, still unknown composer who is poor and leads a band in a night club. We see him enter the lobby of the club and give his coat to the pretty young hat check girl. While he conducts the orchestra in one of his nice waltzes, the girl listens enthralled. She takes the cloak of the composer down from the rack and dances with it as though it were the young man himself.

The flight of birds must have fascinated prehistoric man in many ways, but it seems that the main source for his interest is a sexual one. The fact that a bird can elevate itself by its own power and fly, must have led primitive man and man of antiquity to the comparison of this ability with the erection of his penis. The phallic stone symbols of Mesopotamia wear wings, and the painting on the walls of bordellos evacuated in Pompei show the winged penis. The vulgar Viennese expression for sexual intercourse is *"vögeln"* (to do as the birds) with obvious allusion to the erection of the penis. This mysterious power, transferred from birds to men, still emerges not only in sexual metaphors and symbols. Yahweh says that he took the Israelites "on eagles' wings" from Egypt. The other day a music critic expressed in a beautiful image, the power of Mozart's music: One feels as though one were touched by the flutter of angels' wings.

Of a similar symbolic origin as the cloak must be the hat of women because it often appears in their dreams as substitute for the male genitals. Also the language confirms this unconscious sexual significance. The German expression *"unter die Haube kommen"* means, literally translated, to get under a cap. It signifies getting married or to get a husband because only married women were allowed to wear a cap while girls had none. It is interesting that the same sexual significance has to be attributed to the hat in the unconscious productions of men. The democratic spirit of America shows itself also in the fact that no man takes his hat off to another man.

The German writer Abraham Gotthelf Kastner (1719-1800) who was professor of mathematics in Göttingen and also published poems and political essays wrote the following "Lament of a Woman at the destruction of French fortifications at Göttingen" (1763):

> Here where once were seen myriads
> Of long thick palisades
> Stuck in narrow holes, deeply cleft,
> Now only empty, enlarged holes are left.

The epigram, written almost two hundred years before psychoanalysis, identifies consciously Mother Earth with a symbolic representative of the female body.

Personification of the male genital is ubiquitous and pervades all layers of communication. A patient called her husband "mister," and his penis "master" and asked him upon certain occasions "Is the master at home?" meaning jokingly whether or not he had an erection and wished to make love to her. Goethe, in one of his poems, gave the name Ipse (he himself) to the penis. In a letter to her lover a girl wrote, "I am longing for you and him."

Here is an example in whose psychoanalytic interpretation the unconscious interplay of sexual symbolism of man and woman could be made transparent. A young woman walked with a friend of her husband on the street. He continued to woo her ardently. While she listened silently to his passionate words, she smoked a cigaret. At a certain point the man stumbled and almost fell down. The young woman who was trying to help him up took the cigaret out of her mouth. When she put it in again, it was with the burning end turned around so that she hurt her tongue. We have here a combination of slips which shows that the unconscious of the two persons understood each other. In this subterranean communication the slip of the man as well as that of the woman are compromise-actions in which their desires and the self-punishments for them come to a simultaneous expression. The young man had unconscious scruples against entering a sexual affair with the wife of a man whom he liked and admired. The young woman expressed her unconscious counter-will opposing sexual relations with the man in her mistake. The cigaret functions here as a sexual symbol. The stumbling of the man amounts unconsciously to a self-warning.

Occasionally a wit shows that the sexual symbolism, emerging in our dreams, is also used in this joking form. A woman said in her psychoanalytic session: "It is with the sexual arousal of men as with those new automatic elevators. It is all much too quick. You scarcely come near to them, and they already ascend and you have scarcely arrived at a certain floor, they immediately go down."

Another sexual symbol is to be found in Stendhal's *The Red and the Black*. Mr. de Renal says with a coarse laugh: "There you have women. There is always something out of order in their machinery." The same view was expressed by a Serbian peasant who told me, during the First World War: "With a woman it is as with a watch, there is always something to repair." (What men do not add is that this fragile and delicate machinery appears to be superior in a biological sense to the male organism. Biologists agree that men have less resistance than women to every major killer disease except diabetes. It is well-known that women in general live longer than men. Dr. Edward Bortz came to the conclusion: "Nature apparently places a higher value on the female, the mother of the species, than the male." She can withstand more abuse, possibly because her cellular structure has a greater reserve capacity built into it. It is doubtful if the female of the species is deadlier than the male, but it is certain that she is more equipped to resist the death instinct than he is.)

Men do not have the tendency to put objects which will not be used immediately into receptacles such as bags, boxes, drawers and baskets. Women, however, do. They seem to feel that such things should not be left lying freely around. The reason for such eagerness about putting these objects away, and into receptacles, is often given as orderliness or neatness. The editor of the New Yorker magazine, Ross, used to rage:* "It's the only office in the world where paste and scissors are kept in desk drawers. The women do that. And if they don't show up for work, you can't ask why." It is not difficult to guess some of the unconscious motives expressed in the feminine habit here described. In vulgar slang, the vagina is called "box."

Freud pointed out that even the kinds of suicide men and women prefer show a concealed sexual symbolism. Men most frequently hang or shoot themselves, while women prefer poison or drowning. In the suicide of men, the reference to the male genitals is still recognizable. (The revolver as penis-substitute—the erection in hanging.) The drowning in a woman's suicide, still alludes to pregnancy (the intrauterine life of the embryo surrounded by water), also the poisoning alludes to impregnation.

The symbol of the house for the woman can be found again in a recent good movie, *Marty:* a woman whose son had left her to marry, warns her woman-friend whose son is still single and shares an apartment with her, that he too will leave her for a girl. The woman tells her friend that the first sign for such unconscious intentions on the part of the son will be dissatisfaction with the apartment he shares with his mother. Soon after this conversation, the son, who is still single but has recently become very attracted to a certain girl, comes home and finds fault with the old and shabby apartment in which he lives with his mother. It is very doubtful if the author who wrote the script of the movie,

* James Thurber, *The Years with Ross*, Boston, 1957.

knew that the old house was a symbolic representation of the mother.

This last example offers an opportunity to point to the biological pattern that determines the sexual symbolism of the house or the apartment. To make a home or an apartment comfortable is as natural to a woman as it is to a bird to build a nest. Nest building is, so to speak, the instinctive pattern process after which interior decorating and homebuilding are moulded. In making a home for her mate, woman continues the preparation of her body for the unborn baby whose predecessor is his father.

The unconscious equation of the room and the woman's body reaches further than she knows. The other day, a woman explained to me why she chose small chairs and tables for a certain room in preference to larger ones: the smaller furniture would make the room appear larger. This same principle operates when a woman chooses a hat or a dress (if she is wise), or even the design of a wallpaper. Men, with the exception of interior decorators, rarely think in such terms about rooms and furniture. It appears to be alien to most men to see rooms as substitutes for their bodies.

For women the apartment is not only the place they live in, but that they live with. Every spot in it is filled with memories of events in their lives and in the lives of those near and dear to them. Those memories are in their thought so intimately connected with certain places within the apartment that they are brought to mind in correlation with them. Men in general do not think in those local terms when they bring memories to the surface. The unconscious equation of room and woman's body is often confirmed by women themselves. A woman speaking of curtains for the dining room compared the situation of a person passing and looking into the uncurtained room with that of a peeping Tom who sees a woman undressed. Here is an indirect confirmation of my statement* that curtains have for women the unconscious symbolic significance of underwear covering the windows (as unconscious genitals-symbols).

A prepsychotic patient complained about her refrigerator whose state worried her. In her complaints she called the refrigerator ice-box. Her husband had not approached her sexually for several years.

The unconscious symbolism is extended to furniture and other parts of the room. This feminine attitude can sometimes help to explain a seemingly irrational behavior puzzling to men. A woman refused to use the bed-linen her predecessor in marriage had left. The husband was a widower whose first wife had died several years ago, but the new wife energetically rejected his suggestion to use the linen with the first wife's monogram. She said, "It is as if you would still sleep with her." The husband considered this statement only fanciful.

My knowledge of the newest psychoanalytic literature is limited. I can thus not venture to state that the same sexual symbolism that emerges in dreams was proved in all fairy tales. I am fairly certain that the shoe that fits only Cinderella was analytically interpreted as the vagina best fitted for the prince's penis (foot). I don't know if the hedge of thorns surrounding the Sleeping Beauty was conceived as hymen and its piercing as deflowering. A surprising finding in the field of sexual symbolism in a fairy tale was provided by the comparison of a dream-element with a part of the Snow White story. The dreamer dreamed of an omnipotent dwarf

* In *Of Love and Lust*, New York, 1957.

who could transform himself into other forms. In her thought-associations the name Wistik occurred. This is the name of a magical dwarf who plays an important role in Frederick van Eeden's novel *De Kleine Johannes*. The dreamer, a Dutch woman, had read this book a short time ago. The almighty dwarf who could adopt various forms made her think of the male genital. The ensuing thoughts led her to reminiscences of Walt Disney's picture, *Snow White and the Seven Dwarfs*. She had seen this dramatized fairy tale a short time ago. Suddenly she began to laugh because she remembered a scene from the movie in which Snow White danced with each of the dwarfs. The number seven made her think of the number of days in a week. On this detour she arrived at the thought that Snow White of the seven dwarfs was fortunate to have daily sexual intercourse.

A patient whom I tried in vain to convince that his recurring writer's cramp reflected some sexual difficulties he often experienced found a surprising confirmation of this strange view. He once spoke with an old aunt (who had certainly never heard anything about sexual symbolism) about a young girl. The aunt praised the girl while the young man spoke derogatively about her. The aunt looked at him and said smilingly, "I am sure you have already written on worse paper than this."

INTERLUDE

"Pretty warm for May, isn't it?" I said. George and I had walked along Riverside Drive from Seventy-second to Ninety-second Street. "Let's go down there and sit on a bench near the river. It's much cooler near the water."

"Fine," he said, "although I had the impression that you almost shivered with chill when I described my experiments." George, who is almost ten years younger than I, is head of the psychology department of a Midwestern university. For the last half-hour he had tried to interest me in experiments he had made and which should demonstrate certain psychological divergencies in the color- and tone-perception of his male and female students. "I know, of course, that you don't think highly of the experimental branch of psychology, but I imagine that you are studying those basic differences yourself."

"If it amuses you to plan and perform those experiments, I am only too pleased, but I doubt that they will cast a light on the fundamental sexual distinctions. Yet I can imagine some kind of experiments which comes closer to the core of the problem."

"Such as . . . ?" asked George. "I would tell you," I said, "if it were not so fantastic that it will arouse your sarcasm."

"I have heard plenty of fantastic things from you, my dear Theodor, for instance some psychoanalytic theories. If you promise not to call up the spirit of lamented Sigmund Freud, I will listen with great attention."

"The experiment I thought of has certainly nothing to do with psychoanalysis. It started as a kind of scientific daydream. It can never be performed in reality. Let me start from the first premise for any experiment. It should be made in as much isolation as possible and under the most favorable circumstances. Is this not correct?"

"Correct. Please come to the point!"

We sat down. I felt much better.

"Now, let's return to my imaginary experiment! Let's face the music. Here is the situation: The psychologist who wants to compare the two sexes sees his subject only 'in mixed company.' "

"I am a poor soul, lost in the dark."

"It's simply this: you, a man, observe women as they behave and act when they are in company of a man. Imagine now the following case: a man, a trained psychological observer, succeeds in living, let's say for many months, unrecognized as a man only amongst women. He is dressed as a woman, behaves like a woman—as far as a man can do that— and no one doubts that he is a female."

"He would not be in an enviable situation. . . . If I am not mistaken, Hercules had to live as a woman among women for three years. I don't know at the moment if this was not also one of his twelve labors. It was, at all events, a Herculean task."

"It was certainly not for the purpose of psychological observation," I said.

"Granted the bizarre premise of your suggested experiment, what is its aim? What do you want to prove?" George asked.

"It should answer some important preliminary questions. It has the character of an expedition of reconnaissance into an unexplored territory. One of those precursory problems is for instance the one from which we departed: how much is the behavior of women changed in the company of men? How do they behave when they are amongst themselves?"

"Do you think they are only secrets of their toilette and hygiene or do you mean that they speak differently to each other and so on?"

"I thought in the first line of the changed view at which a male observer would arrive under these circumstances. He would decidedly alter his concept of femininity when he could look at women amongst themselves. He would get rid of many conventional and even of a few scientific preconceived ideas. He would for instance discover that women are basically much more alike than he thought before and more things than are only dreamt of in your philosophy or psychology."

George admitted this. "No doubt," he said, "Some of his experiences would convince him that girls are not only made of sugar and spice. Some new insights he would gain will perhaps sober him and make him immune to romance. He might at the end agree with that malicious Bernard Shaw who thought that to fall in love with a woman means to overestimate the difference between one woman and the other."

I thought that over and said, "He would, at all events, experience many surprises. Some pleasant ones too, for instance he would discover that women have a special delicacy of feeling and that they often develop a kind of sisterly and helpful attitude towards each other."

"I can imagine that," George remarked. "Your experimenter will after a few months of mixing only with womenfolk have an urgent desire for the company of men, if only to compare notes with them about the psychology of women."

"Possible. But mind you, my imaginary experiment is not yet finished with the report in which the psychologist will summarize his findings after his return from his voyage of exploration. A second expedition will be organized. This time a female observer, equally well trained, will have to live for many months disguised as a man amongst men only. Don't you think that the views of this woman about men, about their habits and customs, will be also considerably altered?"

"Sure, but you forget that this kind of experiment has

been conducted many times in reality. Admitted, not as an experiment, but for reasons of expediency, determined by war and exceptional labor-conditions. Think only of nurses and female army-corps during the last year. . . . By the way, it just occurs to me that you did not take into account how the validity of your experiment will be endangered by the influence of the sexual factor. Neither the male nor the female observer are unaffected living with the other sex, both are only human. How about the temptations of the flesh?"

"Well, we assume the ideal case that sexual desires would not interfere with the objectivity of their observations."

"You are admirably naïve, Theodor. Apropos women living with men: there is nothing new under the sun. Did not Joan of Arc live with the soldiers in the war dressed as a man? It occurred to me just now what I read the other day. In her trial at Rouen several colonels who shared their tents with her during the whole campaign attested that they had never felt the temptation to approach her sexually. None of those ruffians experienced the very human desire to rape the maid and they all considered this unusual lack of sexual temptation genuine proof of her holiness. I hope for the sake of the salvation of your soul that you share their conviction."

"Let's not be diverted by anecdotes, George! I assert that living exclusively in men's society would also change woman's opinions of men to some extent. She would, for instance, be shocked by the coarseness and brutality of men, she would perhaps admire their singleness of purpose and other qualities. At all events, here is the second of my preliminary problems. I guess that the change of her views on men would be much smaller than of men's opinion on women."

"Why do you assume that?"

"Well, I believe that the Sphinx had a riddle or rather

was a riddle for Oedipus, but he was no enigma for her. Women might sometimes wonder about men, but our sex is certainly no mystery for them." George got up from the bench. "Do you feel sufficiently cooled off now? Let's walk again."

We went back up Riverside Drive. George suddenly stopped as if some new thought had occurred to him. "Say, why should that experiment not be performed by a psychologist who is a hermaphrodite? There must be several in our profession. I just remembered that you once mentioned that one of the delegates in the old Austrian parliament was supposed to belong to that group. You said that one of the representatives, the *enfant terrible* of them, no doubt, once addressed the assembly with the words: 'Ladies and Gentlemen, and you, my dear Stepanovics!' "

PART SEVEN

The Curious and The Curiouser

1. WOMEN'S FEELINGS

A woman says: "When I go home in the night, I am always afraid when I run into a man or a group of men. You never know what they will do. They will perhaps attack you or hit you over the head. I am never afraid of women—not even of the lowest prostitutes in the red-light district. They will perhaps abuse you; the worst they can do is snatch your bag. But I never think they will assault or kill me. Women are here to give life, not to destroy it."

A woman says: "When I ask Anne, my cleaning-woman in Woodstock, 'How was your winter?' she says: 'John was ill.' She need not say more. I know what this means and I imagine what worries she had, when the breadwinner was ill and could not work. I know how worried she was about the children and that she had desperately to run around to get work to feed them. A man to whom she would say, 'John was ill' would not feel what that meant and would say: 'I am pleased that he has recovered.'"

2. OLD AGE

The impoverishment of emotional life for old men is characterized by the emptiness experienced when the vices

of youth have left them and by regrets about missed oppor-
tunities and satisfactions those vices would have offered.
There is often a repentance felt about sins one has missed
committing—thus just the opposite of what our moralists
preach.

Older men looking back on their life and all the furious
fighting and feuding in it sometimes wonder what was it all
about. They occasionally remember that they proudly vowed
"I'd rather die fighting than quit and surrender." And then
they occasionally recognize the whole futility of their strife:
there was nothing to fight. It must have been a sad experience when old Don Quixote sobered and disillusioned finally
understood that he had attacked no knights, but windmills.

LIES

Men perhaps lie as often as women, but they are patheti-
cally amateurish in comparison with the other sex. Some
women get a kind of artistic pleasure in rehearsing in
thought and then verbalizing certain lies they will tell their
husbands or lovers. They enjoy the text as poets do their
lines anticipating their recital. Such women speak the truth
only in emergency situations. Men who enjoy the fabrication
of lies in this way and gleefully imagine the credulity of the
audience are mostly in the category of poets or psychopathic
personalities. The psychological question is here not the
comparison of the ability of deception in both sexes—even
the stupidest woman is in this direction a genius compared
with man—but of the enjoyment of the situation in which
the lie will be told.

There are amongst the lies women tell their husbands or
lovers many which are masked truths. That means they are

darkly perceived potentialities in the women themselves which will become realities later on. All their lies thus become true in time.

3. STRANGER TO ONESELF

The relationship of woman to her mate is so much more intensive than the one of the man to the woman that she often becomes a stranger to herself when the man suddenly changes his attitude to her. She does not understand herself any longer, because she does not see that it is the same man whose love-object she had been.

4. FEMININE FEAR

Most women are secretly afraid of being "found out" by men: that means that they are afraid men will discover that they have wide gaps in their knowledge or intelligence, a restricted ability to understand certain things, a narrow horizon. Many of the maneuvers of women are measures of protection against possible penetration of their pretenses. They are afraid men will discover what is beneath their surface and see their superficiality. They are often aware that their displayed intellectuality covers a false prosperity. In this sense they overappreciate the importance of intelligence as if it were the only or the most important function of the human mind and underappreciate their own qualities like perceptiveness, intuitive understanding, depth and delicacy of feelings.

5. GOVERNMENT

If women would take over the government, if there were stateswomen instead of statesmen, their love-affairs would still be more important than those of the state. It is very likely that their regime would have various forms perhaps even an authoritarian one, but it would never be a regime of terror. Even if they would choose a democratic form of government, the Majesty of Baby would be acknowledged.

6. CLOTH

It is not true that only the French wit is cynical with regard to relations with women. In a cartoon a man is presented in conversation with a friend. He says, "It is not so that only the external appearance of a woman matters; the underwear is also important."

Women are also in their clothing more obedient to the laws of biology than men. An old man might dress himself the same way as his teen-aged grandson. A woman who would wear a dress such as her granddaughter wears would make herself ridiculous.

7. REASON

Women sometimes look at the course and results of man's reasoning in a mixture of tolerance, amusement and serious doubt. Thus Sancho Panza must have listened to some schemes and abstract thoughts of Don Quixote and have been skeptical of all the eccentricity and unreality of the knight's reasoning. Seen from a certain psychological point of view, the opinions of many men appear as stupidity and narrow-mindedness or even insanity, compared with the flexibility women show in their views. The Berlin psychiatrist E. Bonhoeffer once said, "Only the opinions of idiots and policemen are unshakable."

How unfair we men are in our attitude towards women! We want her to give up her vagueness, vagary and instinctive approach and live according to what we consider "reason." At the same time we wish she should remain feminine and we are disappointed if she is adopting masculine manners and codes. It is as if you demand from a child she should act and feel like an adult person, but keep the charm and naturalness of a child. The paradoxical demand woman is confronted with is, "Change, but remain as you are."

8. TEMPORARY ACCEPTANCE

There are certain difficult or critical situations in life which can be conquered only after one has accepted them for the time being in the hope that one's powers or destiny will solve the problem in the future. The Dutch language has for this state of resigned acceptance the expressive phrase "*neerlegen*" which means verbally to lay down or not to be pushed to futile activity. To use a comparison from Holland's recent history: A Dutchman who would run into a street of Amsterdam during the occupation by the Nazis and shout "Down with Hitler!" is not a martyr, but a fool. He will be dead or imprisoned and tortured in a few minutes and his demonstration is as futile as it is senseless. It was much more advantageous to accept for the moment the overwhelming superior power of the Nazis, and work underground towards their future defeat and expulsion. In the same sense certain intolerable marriages or professional situations have to be accepted until the time is ripe for radical changes either by new insight and with renewed energy of the individual or with the help of favorable circumstances. One has to take those situations from there and hope for the best. Also a strong wish, nurtured a long time, is an emotional power working in the direction of changes.

9. MALE FEAR

Nothing is more dangerous to a satisfactory emotional and sexual relationship of a man to a woman than if he is afraid of her. Being frightened of her can bring him to desperate and violent reactions that are more destructive than hate. Being afraid of a woman is experienced by a man as much more humiliating and damaging to his self-esteem than being her slave.

10. DAY AND NIGHT

The characterization of married life is only half accomplished if everyday existence together is not described in terms of day and night. I would like to compare the words a mother speaks to her son in Goethe's *Hermann und Dorothea* with a definition of marriage by Maupassant almost a century later. In Goethe's lines, the mother encourages her son to marry the girl with whom he has fallen in love:

> Dass dir werde die Nacht zur schöneren
> Hälfte des Lebens
> Und die Arbeit des Tag's dir freier
> und eigner werde

> So that the night will become life's
> more beautiful half
> And the work of the day will be freer
> and more your own

For Maupassant marriage is an exchange of bad humors during the day and of bad odors during the night! *"Des mauvaises humeurs pendant le jour, et des nauvaises odeurs pendant la nuit."*

11. MOMENT OF TRUTH

A patient who came to psychoanalytic treatment because of a long-lasting depression went through a phase in which the intense hostility against her husband was expressed in the sharpest way. Her criticism of the spouse of which she had been unconscious now manifested itself in malicious mockery. Her desire to take revenge on him for many wrongs and hurts to her pride broke through in long spun-out designs of inflicting injuries on him—of abusing and cursing him. Once, in the middle of such explicit and detailed aggressive and insulting outpours she said, as though astonished at her own maliciousness and cruelty: "I really am a bitch!" The psychotherapist remained silent. He followed thus not only the principles of psychoanalytic technique, but also the advice, "Never contradict a lady!"

12. FEMININE LOGIC

Some of the tasks of the psychologists of the future will be to provide us with a textbook of feminine logic. Such an introduction into women's ways of thinking would convince any man that feminine logic *is* unfailingly logical in spite of its seeming illogicality. You have only to accept a few extraordinary premises and then you will have to acknowledge the correct reasoning of the feminine mind. For instance the principle that opposites do not exclude each other or the fact that $2 + 2 = 4$ does not mean it cannot be sometimes 5 or 6 and so on. There is for instance the principle of simultaneity which men don't seem to understand. "Where are the nail scissors? They are not on the dressing table," says the husband. "Of course not," answers his wife. "They are in my bathing suit. Where else would they be?" "In your bathing suit?" "Didn't I tell you that I will go to the beach this afternoon? I will, of course, take the nail scissors with me."

13. The Need To Be Admired

The need of women to be admired is not always very discriminating. A woman felt slightly disappointed when the street cleaner whom she regularly passed by on her way to the office once did not look after her. Her husband asserted that she is hurt if a male dog doesn't wag its tail when she approaches him.

There is sometimes a secret conflict going on between that wish to be admired and the demands of feminine shame. Often the wish that one's beauty will fill the onlooker with delight remains victorious. Would the Venus of Milo be embarrassed if she knew that her nude figure is looked at by millions of men? I seriously doubt it, especially if she were certain that her perfect figure is appreciated by them. She would perhaps regret very much that her statue had no arms and would consider it a pity that those millions of men could not see them in their full beauty. A perfect figure is an excellent guarantee against an extreme feeling of shame.

14. Overappreciation

The moral relativity and insignificance of murderous wishes in us becomes best recognizable when compared with

the self-punishments and exaggerated atonements which neurotics inflict upon themselves. No earthly court would con-
demn a murderer to the severe and barbaric punishments that
obsessional neurotics impose upon themselves. A patient of
mine had a moment of truth in which he clearly recognized
this emotional situation. Many of his neurotic symptoms had
the character of self-punishment for repressed aggressive
impulses. Fenced in by his obsessions, he had condemned
himself to full social isolation, to a kind of solitary confinement of many years intensified by multiple compulsive rituals
which filled his days and did not allow him any rest. They
amounted to a kind of forced labor. Once he said in an
analytic session, "How I torture myself! All these punishments for a few people I killed in thoughts! When one thinks
of the millions of people who perished in the war, their number does not even come into consideration."

15. Don Quixote

A female counterpart of Don Quixote is impossible because women are realists. The horse on which a Don Quixote
of our time rides is not called Rosinante, but Principle.
Even the ladies who are passionate riders would not mount
such a horse, but men ride one every day.

16. Mother-in-Law

For many young wives the mother-in-law is an object of
fear and for many young husbands an object of warning, a
signal reminding them that their wives could once become
similar to their mothers. Some young husbands whose wid-
owed mothers-in-law live with the young couple often think

that the burning of the widows in ancient India was a very reasonable institution.

17. FIVE-FINGER EXERCISE

I once observed a young woman while she followed with great, but well-concealed interest the flirtatious behavior of a girl who was in vivid conversation with a man. The observant girl was obviously very aware of the words, gestures and glances of the other woman. Her great concealed attention seemed not to be spontaneous and had almost an automatic character. The situation reminded me of another one: During the performance of some Haydn-quartets I happened to sit beside a well-known musician who had once been concert master in an orchestra. While the man listened to the instrumentalists, he automatically moved his fingers as if he had a violin in his hands on which he himself played.

18. A SLIP IN READING

A patient read Shaw's *Man and Superman* and in it the sentence that marriage combines "the maximum of temptation with the maximum of opportunity." The patient, who had been married for more than twenty years, misread the line as "the minimum of temptation with the maximum of opportunity," and recognized only later on that this was only correct in her own personal case.

19. SEMANTIC PROBLEM

During an amiable discussion on the meaning of words a member of a semantic society called me "anti-semantic." I had asserted that the science of semantics leaves many important problems outside the range of its attention. Here are two of them: why are men using words women avoid and why are women using expressions not to be found in the conversations of men? Every research into this problem will result in psychological comparisons. Here is another problem unexplored by semantics: Why do most developed languages make a difference between woman and girl, Frau und Mädchen, femme and jeune fille? Why, in contrast with this differentiation, are different names only rarely used for married man and bachelor? Should not from this divergence the conclusion be drawn that marriage is of paramount importance for the woman while it has a minor role in the life of a man?

20. AMERICAN AND FRENCH WOMEN

The differences between American and French women seem to be that American women are much more independent than their sisters in France and that their attitude towards men is in general less amenable than that of French women. I do not venture to decide if there is a causal connection between those two facts, and would prefer to quote one of our Hollywood stars who spent some time in Paris and was interviewed about those differences. The lady said, "American women are charming to each other but nasty to men, and French women are charming to men but nasty to each other."

21. BLAST TO HELL

A social worker in her thirties, virginal and rather homely, who worked in a clinic, came for analytic treatment because she was tortured by sudden anxieties in the presence of people important to her in her profession, or sometimes even at occasions that were just of a social nature. At staff meetings in her hospital those anxieties often acquired a panic-like character and she had to leave the room. She could give me no information about the content of her anxiety, which puzzled herself. She could not tell me of what she was afraid nor what conditioned the emergence of sudden anxiety-attacks. The first insight I could obtain was gained by the deciphering of a dream. She dreamed: *I am with the psychiatrists and the psychologists to discuss a case. Suddenly I do not know if I had turned off the gas or not. All persons present are looking pale as wax. I am opening the windows. I am terrified and leave. At home I was afraid of what could have happened to them.* The ensuing interpretation of this dream left no doubt about its significance: the patient was often tortured by gas-pains and was sometimes worried that she could not control herself and would let go. The intense shame and embarrassment at the thought that the persons present in the room would sense the bad odor and guess that it came from her was unconscious and was not recognized by her as the cause of the anxiety she experienced. The dream presents this possibility as realized and depicts in sensational and grotesque exaggeration the effects of her flatulence. It is easy to guess that the patient had strong unconscious aggressive tendencies against the psychiatrists and psychologists in her clinic. Without being aware of it she expresses her sharp criticism in impulses to release gas. We know from a great number of clinical experiences that such impulses of release gas are an unconscious expression of scorn and contempt. The emotional reaction against the temptation was the intense anxiety that appeared in her suddenly and mysteriously in situations in which she experienced unconscious tendencies of the described kind.

22. THE TWO BASIC TEMPTATIONS

In the light of psychoanalytic findings it should be possible to define the basic temptations with which men and women in our culture-pattern have to wrestle. In order not to succumb to them society has developed most severe repressions, but was compelled to leave certain loopholes. Those most intensive urges are for men to murder and for women to surrender to prostitution. Clinical experiences in psychoanalysis prove that these temptations are ubiquitous in the repressed fantasies of men and women of our civilization.

We also know the various legalized loopholes to be found in the wall erected against these temptations. The drives impelling mankind to murder and violence find an outlet in capital punishment within an organized society and in wars against other groups. To the temptation luring women to prostitution not only those women succumb who submit to sexual intercourse for gain, but also the others who marry for money.

PART EIGHT

Complexes and Complexities

---

1. LITERARY ASSOCIATIONS

I am astonished that in the books and articles on psycho-analytic interpretation, literary thought-associations of the analyst play such an insignificant part. Except in the works of Freud, reminiscences of scenes from novels and plays as well as lines from poems are very rarely mentioned as leading to or helping in the interpretation of dreams or neurotic symptoms. In my experience literary associations serve as valuable "leads" and sometimes as direct tracks to the understanding of unconscious processes. Alone they can rarely solve the problem dreams or neurotic formations present, but their emergence is a meaningful help in tracing unconscious thoughts. They operate like bloodhounds leading our thoughts to the trail of the hidden significance of unconscious processes. Here are a few examples: A middle-aged man had several sexual affairs with the wives of older men who were his admired and highly appreciated teachers. He complained about a strange symptom: he sometimes had the sensation as he undressed to go to sleep that he would find that he no longer had a penis. In continuing his thoughts in this direction he spoke of a fear he had often had as a little boy, namely that a dog would bite off his genital. The literary thought-association occurring to me at this moment was the

memory of two lines from a Spanish ballade Heinrich Heine
once quoted; in it a knight lies chained in a prison which is
infested by rats. He complains: *"Ach, sie fressen, ach, sie
fressen womit meistens ich gesündigt."* ("Oh, they eat, oh,
they eat that which I have sinned most with.")

Another instance: a patient at the end of his forty years
who had lived a sexually ascetic life for several years had
found a special method to overcome sensual temptations.
Whenever he feels intensively aroused, he quickly undresses
and jumps under an ice-cold shower. While he described this
procedure in an analytic session, the name of Saint Francis
of Assisi occurred to me and with it the memory of an
anecdote Anatole France once told about the Pater Seraphi-
cus.* In the middle of a very cold winter the saint experienced a violent attack of sexual temptation. He tore his
clothes and rolled nude in the snow-covered roses and thorns
of the convent garden. The roses, sprinkled with the saint's
blood, miraculously arose and blossomed. Since then the
roses of that garden have dark spots on their petals as tokens
of the victory of St. Francis over the Evil One. The nuns sell
these stigmatized roses still, and Anatole France bought some
and wore them as a talisman near his heart, as he told his
young secretary. He adds that they did not, alas, protect him
against the temptation of the flesh as well as they did St.
Francis.

Here is a dream in whose interpretation a literary reminis-
cence proved very helpful: a middle-aged woman reports the
following dream: "I kiss a bird and I think he is all wet."
No thought-associations of the patient contributed to illumi-
nate the latent content of the dream. While the patient spoke

* Jean Jacques Brousson, *Anatole France en pantoufles*, Paris, 1924.

of other things, mysteriously the balcony-scene from "Romeo and Juliet" occurred to me: does Juliet there not compare her lover with a bird?

(Act II, scene II.) Here are her lines:

> 'tis almost morning I would have thee gone;
> And yet no further than a wanton's bird,
> Who lets it hop a little from her hand,
> Like a poor prisoner in his twisted gyves
> And with a silk thread plucks it back again,
> So loving-jealous of his liberty.

Romeo: I would I were thy bird.
Juliet: Sweet, so would I.

It occurred to me later that the bird appears in many dreams as a sexual symbol of the male genital and sometimes according to the unconscious equation of this part with the very person as man. (Compare the section on sexual symbols in this book.) Juliet's comparison of the lover with a bird is thus unconsciously determined by this ubiquitous symbolism.

The train of thoughts following the dream present not only a confirmation of this interpretation, but provided the material for the understanding of the other part of the dream. The patient reports that she and her lover were on the preceding evening at a party. In the conversation her lover under the influence of alcohol expressed some political views which she, the patient, considered utterly mistaken or silly. She felt ashamed of him while she kissed him good night. Telling me about the exchange of ideas (to use an exaggerated phrase) among the men, the patient said, "That bird argued . . ." and again "That other bird said . . ." choosing the American colloquialism for this man. It is easy to guess that she used also a colloquial expression in the dream for her view that her lover's political opinions are utterly mistaken ("all wet").

It rarely happens that a psychoanalyst's thoughts lead him from observations and experiences of his daily practice to works of literature, especially to fiction. Several books and papers of Freud and of the psychologists of the post-Freud era bear witness that certain clinical experiences call forth literary research.

Here is an idea stimulated by psychoanalytic consultation, an example of a research project belonging to the area of history of literature, and originated in the insight gained from the observation of a paranoia patient. During the consultation the young man told me that he had been a professional dancer and had been wounded during the last war. Discharged from the navy, he gets a small monthly payment from the government. He asserted that in Washington, D.C. two great parties are engaged in a long and serious conflict on behalf of him. The one party within the government is convinced that he is one of the most gifted dancers and wants to increase his pension to enable him to finish his studies in order to have a glorious future. The other party is hostile to him and wants to destroy him by reducing his pension, by interfering with his personal affairs (also with his relationships with women) and to make his career impossible. There is no necessity to discuss here the syndrom of the patient and to present his case history. After he left me, my train of thoughts led me to a certain form of novel with a typical plot and to reflections on a phase of history of literature. The type of novel in question is called *"Bildungsroman"* in German (novel of growth or development). The essential plot of this novel-type is the following: in its center is a young man whose development from boy to maturity and productive manhood is depicted. His professional uncertainties and entanglement, his mistakes and doubts, his love affairs are followed from boyhood to manhood when he finally recognizes his true vocation and finds a congenial mate. The characteristic feature of this novel form, to be found in numerous variations, is that a secret society of benevolent and wise men follows the development of the young hero, guides him who is not aware of it, protects him in dangerous situations and finally leads him to creativity and redemption. The secret society has different forms, sometimes a character similar to that of freemasons, sometimes of a philanthropic or philosophical association. It is especially concerned with the problem of how the young man attains, led by them, his goals. In a few forms of this novel of growth the secret society has to fight an opposite society that wants to frustrate the leading character and to see him fall. The trials and errors of the young man of whom the secret society takes care are often presented as tests which should prove his worth and his courage. It is easy to follow the course of this novel-type from the middle of the eighteenth century to the present. The leading character is in most cases a poor or middle-class young man who is passionate and ambitious. The secret society is obviously moralistic or humanitarian. Charles Dickens' *Great Expectations* is perhaps the best-known representative example of this type in England. Goethe's *Wilhelm Meister* and Schiller's *Geisterseher* are the most famous and most influential novels of this kind. Mozart's *The Magic Flute* follows in its plot the same typical trend.

The interesting aspect of the literary problem, posed here, is, of course, the psychological question of why and how this kind of novel emerges and what is its unconscious meaning. Its connections with paranoid fantasies of grandeur and of persecution as well as the unconscious homosexual tendencies with regard to father-representative figures (the secret society) are obvious. As in the fantasies of my patient about the two opposite parties in Washington, the figure of the father-representative to whom the son-character had origi- nally an ambivalent attitude, is divided into two parts: a kind and benevolent one in the form of the secret society and a malicious, dangerous and persecutory one, formed by its antagonist. The psychological significance of this kind of division, similar to that in the symptoms of paranoic patients, will be one of the key-problems of psychological exploration that will best be conducted by a psychoanalyst familiar with and interested in the history of literature. Too old and too preoccupied with other research-projects, this writer can only recommend the highly interesting subject to the attention of young analysts. Here a beautiful, unsolved problem awaits its examination by a scholar of the young generation.

2. VANITY OF THE MARTYR

How far ahead in psychological insights are many creative writers compared to us psychoanalysts! We needed years of work and clinical experience to arrive at the definite analytic concepts of social masochism which were anticipated by Gustave Flaubert in his *Tentation de Saint Antoine* in 1875. The saint in Flaubert's reconstruction considers all he has endured during his life in the desert. In his soliloquy he reflects on all he has suffered. "I have spent more than thirty years in the desert. I have burdened myself with thirty pounds on my back as Eusebius; I surrendered my body to the insects as Maccarius, I have spent fifty-three nights without closing the eyes as Pachomius. Those who are decapitated, those whom they tweak with tongs and whom they burn have perhaps less merit than I because my life is a perpetual martyrdom."

Not only the vanity and vainglory in the martyrdom is here demonstrated, but also the never-ceasing competitiveness of the anachoretic saint with other martyrs and his ambition to surpass them in sufferings. Psychoanalysis needed almost a hundred years (compare my book *Masochism in Modern Man*) until its explorations rediscovered the unconscious trends in martyrdom which Flaubert has anticipated in his characterization of Saint Anthony.

3. THE MYSTERY OF SEX

One of the decisive incentives of male sexuality is the urge to denude the female and to discover her secret, the hidden genitalia. One wonders what would happen, if all women would again walk around naked. Would half of mankind suddenly be turned into a nudist camp? One could predict that in a short time the intensity and urgency of male sexuality would, to a considerable extent, be reduced. It does not need too great an imagination to invent such a possibility which would form an interesting counterpart to the scenes Anatole France described in *L'Ile des Pinguins*. In that memorable report about primal times Saint Mael sits near the sea and sees a monk called Magis bringing clothes for the natives of the island Alka who had until then known only their birthday costume. Magis, whose features were appropriated by the devil, warned the old saint that the consequences of giving cloth to the Penguins would be serious indeed. "Today," he says, "when a Penguin covets a Penguin woman, he knows what he desires and his concupiscence is limited by the precise knowledge of the desired object."

He foresees that when the Penguin women were clothed, the male would not be clear about what attracts him to them and his desire would pour forth in daydreams and fantasmagorias. The Penguin females will cast down their eyes and make believe that they conceal a treasure below their covering. In the following scene the monk grabs a Penguin woman who is uglier than the others, and dresses her, thus transforming her in the eyes of the natives—but also in his own eyes—into a mysterious object of desires. She is later followed by all males who see her. The female dances away, moving her hips, well aware of her new appeal. Magis points out to the saint how all Penguins stare as if fascinated at the middle part of the young woman. The charm of the female figure is the more increased since the Penguins, instead of clearly seeing it, are compelled to present it to themselves in imagination. They feel that if they could hold her buttocks in their hands, they would embrace the climax of human lust. When the old Saint Mael walks to his hermitage he already sees six- or seven-year-old Penguin girls who have made girdles for themselves out of seaweed and who run across the beach glancing back to see if men were following them.

It is not difficult to imagine scenes that would undo the miracle here described, scenes that would transform the modern world in a not too Rousseau-like *"retour à la nature."* A modern successor of the Saint Mael who is convinced that male concupiscence is intensified by the secrecy of the female body concealed in dresses would compel woman to walk about naked again. Sexual desire would, of course, remain and run its course, but after some time it would lose its exaggerated intensity and return to the limitations that were transgressed by civilization. The stimulus of the mysterious and the attraction of the hidden, powerful components of male sexual urges would in this case be abolished. The modesty of the woman would be reduced to the extent it appears in Australian savage tribes. With those changes one of the factors that pull men to bring it down and to conquer female resistance would disappear. But would the world of sexuality not be impoverished by the absence of the mysterious? The fascination of the unknown would at least be weakened in its intensity.

4. Gestures and Glances

There are glances, movements, gestures and postures characteristic of one sex, and seldom observed in the other. We would hardly say of a man that he gave a woman the "glad eye." A man but rarely casts covert glances at a girl, he looks directly at her. One might observe a couple walking down the street, talking. You will usually find that the man looks ahead and but rarely looks at the woman while she speaks. Yet she will often glance at him out of the corner of her eye. This quick glance, through half-closed eyes, is rarely observed in men, but frequently in women. Who has ever seen a man, curled up on a chair with his feet under him? Yet women take this position quite often and seem both comfortable and poised in it. Nor have I ever seen a man turn around and scrutinize his back. Yet women are quite preoccupied with this area, wondering if their skirt is mussed or their stockings crooked. Perhaps even a run has started, all unobserved without this decorative contortion. We often see a man stalking around the room, up and down, with his hands behind his back as he thinks; or standing quietly with arms crossed. Only once, I believe, have I seen a woman in either of these positions and she was imitating a man at this time.

Physiological, as well as psychological and esthetic factors favor a certain posture in one sex and prevent it in the other. I have had occasion to observe boys on their way to high school carrying a pile of books; most of them carried them at their side, under the right arm. Yet the girls, walking along side them, carried their books differently—in front of their bodies or near their breasts, and with both arms. I speculated about this and made some psychological deductions. I mistrusted them until I happened upon a mystery story which seemed to confirm rather than deny the thoughts which had passed through my mind. The leading female character, Molly Morrison, is a college girl who walks with a lecturer, carrying many books. While walking beside him she has the feeling that she does not reach his height by half. She presses her books against her breast as though she held a new-born baby. I doubt whether the writer* of this mystery story consciously realized the deeper meaning of the interpretation she gave to this characteristic posture.

There are still experiments to be made in this area of comparative psychology, experiments which would convince every skeptic of the significance of the differences between the sexes. Let us suppose that we ask a woman to describe to us the dress worn by a certain lady at the party yesterday. Then let's ask a man to describe the dress of his neighbor at the party. From the woman, we will get a detailed and full report accompanied by many gestures which illustrate the

---

* Helen Eusis, *The Horizontal Man*. To my regret the American original of the story was not available to me. I read it in French (Paris 1957, p. 9) from which the sentence is quoted: *"Et elle, à côté de lui, avec le sentiment qu'elle n'atteignait pas la moitié de sa taille, pressant ses livres sur sa poitrine comme un bébé tout neuf."*

material, the cut and the lines of the dress. From the man you would get at best a very short gestureless description. Someone asked the other day if it is imaginable that a woman could describe a dress without accompanying gestures, so to speak with her hands tied. The answer quickly given by a woman was "Of course! Women can give each other a full description of a dress in a telephone conversation." But in this case their voice replaces the gestures and vividly depicts or imitates all details of the dress.

It would be worth a psychologist's while to observe, register and describe gestures, positions and glances a man or woman imitates when he or she parodies the behavior of a member of the other sex. It is remarkable that such mocking presentations are much oftener met with men than with women. Homosexual men, for instance, frequently mimic typically feminine gestures and facial expressions for purposes of travesty.

The greater self-awareness women acquire in their double education is not restricted to a few situations. It reaches from the perception that the color of the couch upon which she sits does not offset her dress, to the cautiousness with which she will smile later on so that her mouth is seen at best advantage. It is feasible for a woman to make a gesture of despair and, at the same time, put her hair in order.

Compared to the attitude of the average man, women are certainly more aware of themselves, especially of the effect they create. This becomes apparent in their behavior during an emotional outburst. A student of psychoanalysis described vividly to me the scene created by a neurotic patient during her psychotherapeutic treatment. She behaved in a highly emotional manner: violent gestures and words proclaimed her hostility toward the therapist, upon whom she heaped accusations and insults. The physician let the storm rage patiently, showing no reaction—but listening stoically. Suddenly the patient said in a sober voice: "It doesn't work," and began to talk again in her usual, casual manner. She must have expected the psychiatrist to react to her outburst either with words of retaliation or with expressions of apology or compassion. When she perceived that her maneuver had failed, she was able to return to her previous unemotional position.

In cases such as this, not only the manipulating function of the emotional expression is remarkable, but also the self-control present during the manifestation of seemingly most spontaneous and intense feeling. An objective observer will understand that this control operates even during the outburst and prevents it from becoming excessive and thus losing its effect. The situation in which the psychological observer of such a scene finds himself could be compared to that in a little anecdote which I was told in Vienna. A small boy stood in front of a fountain in a Viennese park, deaf to his mother's pleas to hurry up and come home. He watched, fascinated, the fountain throwing a big spray of water into the basin. "Why on earth don't you come on?" his mother asked, perplexed. His rather unexpected explanation was, "I want to wait until the basin gets filled up and overflows." It seems that, although woman "sprays," she is careful never to overflow. She keeps the big boy, called man, waiting, bewitched and bewildered, while she throws a great scene, at the same time observing his reactions.

5. LEGS

Unbelievers deny that there are miracles possible in these days. Yet who has not seen that a few inches of artificial elevation of women's shoes from the ground can transform a woman in the eyes of a man? High heels render a miracle that transforms the female leg into something which far surpasses the character of a limb.

Women's stockings are usually of lighter colors than the dresses in order to show the beauty of a well-formed female leg to best advantage. At the same time the glance of the man follows the stockings to the hem of the dress beneath which begins for him the mystery of the unknown.

It is generally accepted that high-heeled shoes are for the man more attractive than low-heeled shoes. We know from Freud's analysis of fetishism what are the unconscious reasons for this preference. The sexual attraction exerted by stockings and high heels make it obvious that in the majority of men a kind of leg-fetishism is operating. Women must be unconsciously aware of it; why else would they put their best foot forward?

The expression bluestocking as denoting a woman who is very much interested in literature and science and is at the same time pedantic was first used at the time of Dr. Johnson. If we could make an experiment in thought and if we could imagine that the fashion at this time (more than three hundred years ago) had been the same as today, we would arrive at a likely assumption: even in the most fanatic type of bluestocking lived a secret or disavowed wish to wear the finest seamless nylon stockings.

6. A SAMENESS

Plutarch reports that King Philip of Macedonia (383-336 B.C.), father of Alexander the Great, tried to conquer a woman by hauling her to him against her will. "Let me go," she said, "for when the candle is out, all women are alike." Such candor about their sex is rare with women. It is explained in this particular case by the unwillingness of the woman to yield to the man's desire. In this case she would go to any length to discourage him. Somewhere, deep down, women are convinced that there is not much difference among them. To deceive the onlooker about their basic similarity they want to look as different as possible whether dressed or undressed.

Women rarely get their feelings hurt when a man makes a general statement about women—even if it appears to be derogatory. What woman would be hurt by the remark: "Fraility, thy name is woman" or "La donna is mobile"? Every woman knows that the first phrase is true only to a very limited extent, and each and every one of them also knows how strong a woman can really be, if necessary. Women do not object very much when men call their sex unstable or irrational. Calling them cruel and inscrutable might even flatter them. Wicked invectives and accusations of women in general—if only expressed in moderate form—will not provoke strong objections. But there is one kind of statement which is felt as offensive and deeply injuring to the pride of almost all women—namely that one woman is just like another. Such an opinion deprives woman of the privilege of feeling that she is quite different from all other members of her sex. There is danger for her in the thought that, to her man, she should not appear as incomparable. She wants him to feel that he has chosen her because she has nothing in common with other women. Let men call them worse, or better, than all other women—but, Oh God! not the same! This possibility of a "sameness" in their make-up of all women is experienced by them as the greatest menace.

Rather, a thousand times, a she-devil than one in an army of identical angels! The New York newspapers now announce the opening of a play entitled: "All women are one." The playwright is lucky if he comes out from the opening night unharmed. The female part of the audience might be tempted to stone him. What a title for a play! "One Woman can be all Women" (namely to one man), would be a more appropriate title.

7. On the Psychology of Masochism

Certain forms of masochistic acts and fantasies remain unexplained as long as one does not succeed in tracing the perverted practices, performed or imagined, back to very early infantile patterns. A patient of mine found a great deal of sexual satisfaction in a ritual whose climax was that the naked woman would sit on his face in such a way that he almost suffocated. The infantile model of this ritual was a kind of rough-housing with the younger brother in which the victor sat on the defeated and thus took possession of him. The sexualization and role-reversal much later resulted in that perverted practice. There are many masochistic perverted men who are especially aroused when women sitting on them urinate or defecate on them. This kind of practice is especially incomprehensible if it is not understood as the continuation of or the regression to an infantile stage. When the reversal of roles is undone, as it is necessary in the psychoanalytic interpretation of masochistic practices, that infantile model emerges, namely the wish to soil the woman. The genital-sexual satisfaction is in the perversion replaced by an earlier form in which evacuation was experienced as pleasurable. The return from genital sexuality to that early pattern of evacuation is, of course, accompanied by unconscious tendencies to humiliate and degrade the object. The part of aggressive and sadistic components is on this stage of mature sexuality very clear. Yet it would be misleading to assume that this component within the sexual gratification is the most important character of the perverse action. The primal nature of the tendency to urinate or defecate on the woman is not hostile or degrading—almost the contrary. The baby soils only people he loves. As every nurse of little children will confirm, to defecate or urinate on a person is an infantile token of affection.

At this point the question may emerge why the analogous fantasy or practice is rarely to be found in women. Masochistic practices are in general not very frequent with women, but, if they are present, they don't take the same form. Two reasons come immediately to mind why the "evacuation" form of masochistic fantasy and practice will not emerge as easily in women as in men. The first is, of course, that sadistic and aggressive trends appearing in reversal in masochism are in women in general not as strongly developed as in men so that their elaboration is not needed as urgently as with the male. The regression to the early pattern of evacuation is made difficult for women because the processes of excretion are accompanied by vivid feelings of shame in an earlier phase in girls than in boys. The return to the pre-shame phase meets thus more and greater obstacles than in men.

To round off this section on the psychology of masochism an instance of a fantasy should be quoted in which the patient was aroused by the description of the ceremonial of knighting at the British court: the queen touches the shoulder of the nobleman with a sword and addressed him with his new title "Rise, Lord. . . ."

To the patient this scene appeared as a typical masochistic one: the queen as representing all women performs a slight punishment and by the symbolic act arouses the man sexually, bring about an erection in him. ("Rise, Lord. . . .")

8. EVALUATION OF THE OTHER SEX

The general evaluation of the opposite sex is, individually as well as in different ages, variable. One can, however, assert that it is much more stable with women than with men, and unavoidable oscillations in women's opinion about men are not as wide and as violent as are those of men about the fair sex. Women, so much more realistic in their attitude than men, are not so blinded by romantic love, nor are they as inclined to worship the loved one and then suddenly show violent contempt of the opposite sex. They do not consider men to be angels, but they rarely see in them devils in human form.

The sways and swings of the views of men towards women are astonishingly far-reaching in both directions. The idealization of woman and her degradation can live side by side in the same man in such a manner that one tendency appears to not interfere with the other.

We can take as representative example the man Goethe, who is certainly a lady's man; this also in the sense that he untiringly praised the ennobling power of woman. The peak of woman's idealization is reached in the last verses of his Faust.

Das Unbeschreiblich
Hier ist es getan
Das Ewig-Weibliche
Zieht uns hinan.

Here the ineffable
Wrought it with love;
The eternal womanly
Draws us above.

Gretchen appears in the final scene of the tragedy in the company of the mater gloriosa, so to speak, as an earthly personification of the Holy Virgin who is the all-mother, the most sublimated and sublime image of womanhood. The Eternal Womanly is not only worshipped here, but transfigured—not only idealized, but transformed into an idol.

But there is another aspect to Goethe's view of woman, complementing her worship: a cynical, yes, even a satanic view. In contrast with exalting her, an intensive drive in the direction of mockery and degradation appears in the alter ego of Goethe, projected onto the figure of Mephisto. Contrast the last scene of Faust, his ascent to heavenly regions and his redemption through Gretchen with the scene of the classical Walpurgis Night in which Faust's other self, called Mephisto, chases the lovely evanescent figures of the Lamae and shouts:

"Cursed fate! Men, born to become fools
From Adam down, becozened tools.
Older we grow, who grows wise and steady
Are you not fool enough already?
We know that wholly worthless is this race
With pinched-in waist and painted face.
Naught wholesome in a folk so misbegotten;
Grasp where you will, in every limb they're wrotten
We know it, see it, feel it,
And still we dance whenever the vile jade reel it."

Here is wild rebellion against the sexual power of woman, a revolt against an attraction whose lack of substance and worth is clearly acknowledged. It is as justified to conceive of Mephisto's outcry as the definitive expression of Goethe's view of the eternal womanly as it would be to consider those verses transfiguring woman as his actual view of them. The analytical term of ambivalence is certainly inappropriate in describing the emotional duality as it appears here—and in most men at certain times.

The necessity to deify and worship man is as alien to woman as the urge to degrade him and devaluate him to the extent that he is lower than dust.

PART NINE

Open Secrets

1. OTHER JOYS, OTHER GRIEFS

There are pleasures and satisfactions for women which are not accessible to men, for instance the gratification resulting from the envy of other women when they see you—a woman—in a new and elegant dress. The anticipated envy of young girl friends because one is more popular or has more dates is later continued in the imagined jealousy of other women about a more important or more prosperous husband, a more elegant apartment or more and nicer children. The thought or the fantasy that other women—especially friends—will explode from envy when they see one in a new magnificent dress is not only an immanent part of the satisfaction experienced when a woman is at the mirror before leaving, it is also an added stimulant, something like spice put into a good dish. No woman is insensitive to the expressions on the faces of other women when she enters a room wearing a beautiful dress.

There are on the other hand experiences of grief or sorrows in women not easily understood by men. It needs some effort of the imagination for a man to feel empathy with the grief of a woman who leaves an apartment in which she lived for some years and to share her emotion of mourning at this occasion, especially when she is moving into a

better apartment. Equally difficult for a man to understand
is why his wife cries when she sees her child go to school for
the first time.

2. SEEING ONESELF

A woman, upon leaving a man who has declared his love
for her, will look into the mirror and will find there a new
person. She will look at herself with greater satisfaction and
self-esteem which has been increased by the knowledge of
being loved. If a man, after he has first recognized that he
is loved by a woman, were to look into a mirror at all, he
would find no change in himself. He might even wonder
about the woman's taste. Women think much more frequently, and more easily, about the impression they make
upon others—men or women. This possibility of seeing
themselves with the eyes of others is a special gift to women.
It includes their appearance as well as their morals, it anticipates the opinion men have of them and the gossip of their
best women-friends.

A patient who had been criticized by her lover began to
hate herself after he had gone, and found many faults with
herself. It was as though she had introjected him and then
turned against herself. Such masochistic self-torture, brought
about by the criticism of a woman, is seldom found in men.

There are, in the middle of the day, and while one's
femininity is consciously fully accepted, some sober thoughts
women have about themselves. You do not often hear them,
least of all when you are a man. Here are a few, picked up
from the material of psychoanalytic sessions: A woman sitting
for a long time before the mirror, applying make-up, thinks,
"What a nuisance the whole thing is!" Another woman

while cooking during a great part of the afternoon, preparing her husband's dinner, "All that work for *one* man!" A girl thinking of marriage, "And why should a man work so hard to support me and my children? What have I to offer?"

3. DISCUSSING THE SPOUSE

Men, talking with other men, rarely discuss their wives, while women speak frequently of their husbands to their friends. This seems to be connected with the greater role played by the man in the life of the woman. The part of the woman appears to be less important in the life of the average man. Perhaps the fact that women communicate more easily with each other has some bearing here. Another factor too has to be added; a social tradition in the form of a silent agreement that a gentleman does not talk about his wife or sweetheart with other men.

One of the first American patients I treated in Vienna after the First World War was a typical New Englander, a man in his middle thirties, member of a socially prominent Boston family. In the first week of psychoanalysis, the patient spoke freely of his memories of childhood and adolescence, of school and sport, of life with his brothers, his father and friends. I finally expressed my astonishment about the fact that he had not spoken of his mother. The patient replied: "A gentleman does not discuss his mother or his religion." I succeeded only slowly in breaking down this inhibition and had to repeat the effort when it became obvious that the patient was very unwilling to express complaints about his wife. Shortly after that, I was consulted by several American women from a similar milieu. They did not show the same inhibitions in discussing their fathers and husbands. The situation has changed in the last decades, but women still air their grievances about their husbands and lovers much more easily and freely than do men about their spouses. Men complain about their wives generally not to their friends. They might speak of their wives to bartenders, that is, under the influence of liquor. Women do not need the stimulation of alcohol, which removes inhibition, to express their complaints about their husbands in conversations with their friends.

At the gathering of the "boys" you might occasionally hear an expression such as, "My ball and chain almost didn't let me come tonight," meaning the wife. Also at hen-parties women will sometimes say, "My lord and master wanted to know where I was going." The difference of the expressions, both ironically used, is palpable.

4. SUBLIMATION

As Freud emphasized in his posthumous papers, sexuality is in its nature masculine—even when it is present in women. Among the many questions posed by psychoanalysis in this area the problem of sublimation has to be attacked anew. Sublimation is, according to Freud, a process of libido that consists in the instinct's directing itself towards an aim other than, and remote from, sexual gratification. The accent in this process falls upon the deflection from the sexual aim. It seems to me that sublimation of the coarse sexual drive itself is impossible. Only the part of the ego drive which is fused with the sexual urges is able to be sublimated. The sexual drives, in their organic character can be as little sublimated as the other vital urges of the body—to drink, to eat, to defecate or to urinate. They cannot be deflected from their original aim. Their energy cannot be used in any other way. Romeo, climbing up to Juliet's balcony, is certainly governed by the wish to be sexually united with her, but the energy applied to the process of climbing is, in its nature, determined by properties of the ego drives and as little sexual as would be the ascent of a mountaineer to a peak. In its purest manifestations, the sexual drive is not concerned with the safety and survival of the individual. The mountain cock at mating time does not pay attention to the approach of the hunter and can easily be shot by him. The sexual drive is a biological force as ungovernable as other elementary powers of nature. Karl Kraus once compared the part which morals play in the area of sexuality to the measure applied to master the wild waves of the sea by the Persian King Xerxes: he tried to put them into chains.

5. The Return of the Oedipus-Situation

It is often under many disguises that a memory-trace of the infantile Oedipus-situation suddenly recurs in the life of adult men and women. To a man who was tempted to get into a sexual affair with an older woman, mother of two children, a sentence suddenly came to mind he had often heard from his mother when he was a child, namely, "Look, don't touch!"

A patient, now in her late forties, reports to her psychoanalyst that she had a long phase of promiscuity in her teens. She lived a double life. At home she acted the part of the chaste young girl whose dates with young men were harmless social occasions, theater and concert and parties. In reality she slept with various young men without much discrimination. In these sexual experiences she considered it as a kind of invitation for the man to have sexual intercourse when she stuck her tongue into his mouth. She was convinced that men almost always reacted to this kind of caress appropriately. The young girl, leaving home after dinner to meet one or the other young man used to kiss mother and father good night. When she once on such an occasion said good night to her father, she suddenly felt the strong impulse to put her tongue into his mouth. Then she was miserably shocked. She instinctively recognized the significance of the impulse whose emergence marked the return of incestuous trends from the area of the repressed.

A young woman who had come to New York to study art had rented a furnished room with an old lady she liked. The student became infatuated with a young man who wooed her and urged her to have a sexual affair. She resisted although she was very tempted to yield to his propositions. The time of painful doubts came to an end in a surprising manner. Once when she came home from a date with the young man she found her landlady in the middle of a heart-attack. The girl helped her, giving her the medicine prescribed, made her lie more comfortably and telephoned the physician. She stayed with the old woman until the doctor came and took care of her until the crisis had passed. When she was sure that the patient had recovered, the young woman telephoned her suitor and told him that she would come to his apartment in half an hour. She reported in her analytic session of the next day that her doubts had suddenly vanished after she had taken care of the old landlady and that she had enjoyed her surrender to the man later on. It was obvious that the landlady represented for her a mother figure. In saving her life she had got rid of unconscious guilt-feelings and could yield to her sexual desire.

6. SECRET FEARS

In a session of control-analysis (presentations of cases which young psychoanalysts discuss with older and experienced psychotherapists) I found that the unknown patient, treated by one of my students, must still have untaped areas of resistance in her analytic treatment. The analyst who presented the case to me was a woman in her late thirties and her patient was a young girl. Certain indications seemed to show that the patient had some undisclosed personal objections to her psychoanalyst. I could, of course, not guess what the precise nature of these resistances were, but I advised the analyst to discuss the issue with her patient at the proper psychological moment. The result of that inquiry was discouraging: the patient stated that she liked her analyst and could not think of any criticisms against her. Repeated following attempts to discover the character of those concealed resistances remained fruitless. Yet the impression remained that a hidden resistance blocked the road of the analytic treatment. The analyst insisted that the patient had kept some objection back; the patient again asserted that she was not aware of anything of this kind. In another context the patient said during the same analytic session: "When I left here yesterday, I had a strange thought on my way home. I thought of you. I know that you are not married and I know that you have about eight psychotherapeutic sessions daily. Besides that I have heard that you attend lectures and seminars. What kind of life is hers, I thought, and I was suddenly afraid I could become like you." It is not difficult to conclude that the secret criticisms the patient nurtured against her analyst was that analysis could have the result that the patient's life would become similar to that of the analyst who had no husband nor children and whose life was all work and no play.

7. REPRESSED EMOTIONS

Not only forgotten memories, but also unknown emotions are dug out from the past in analytic sessions. If we may compare this part of the psychoanalytic work with archaeological research we would assert that we not only bring remnants of ancient temples to the light of day, but revive also the religious fervor from the time of the childhood of mankind. Those buried emotions emerge from their subterranean hiding-places in a strange form: they appear either without any connection with a definite content, are displaced by other objects or put into a secondary correlation. Some memories from early years emerge without any emotions.

Here are two representative examples of another kind in which emotions were lost and found again in psychoanalysis, taken from the case of a man and a woman. The excavated emotions were not recognized as such, but appeared as belonging to the present. It was, to resume the previous comparison, as if a prehistorical pot found in the tomb were used as part of a modern kitchen. The feelings which appeared here on the surface have in common that they belong to the prehistorical past of the individual and were at first not acknowledged as fragments of childhood experiences and as estranged parts of the past; of a never remembered, yet not forgotten early phase of life.

The first patient is a man in the forties, a lawyer who had rather serious problems in his social and professional relations. The father of the patient died when the boy was not yet three years old. Only a few fragmentary memories from this time were available, especially from the father's funeral. The patient came back to this great event several times and described the ceremony in the church and at the cemetery. Arrived at a certain point of his description he interrupted himself with a grievous cry: "Jesus, Mary and Joseph!" (The family was devoutly Catholic.) In the context in which this passionate exclamation emerged, it seemed as if the memory of the father's funeral had brought deep mourning up from the underground. This was unlikely since the father had been ill a long time and did not play a considerable role in the boy's life. He did not feel any conscious sense of loss in the past nor was there any manifestation of mourning for the father in the present. Also the circumstances under which the outcry was repeated in a later description of the funeral contradicted the assumption that the patient's words expressed the feelings of the little boy at that occasion. The words were ejected suddenly, as if pushed out by a mysterious power. They sounded genuine enough—yet they were not part of the language otherwise spoken by the patient. Their emotional expression stood in vivid contrast with his otherwise controlled and unemotional voice. The incident remained puzzling until it occurred to me that the words were really not those of the patient, but the outcry he had heard from his mother when her husband's body was buried. The young boy must have felt the deep grief of his mother and without quite understanding the significance of her loss must have identified with her. That exclamation "Jesus, Mary and Joseph!" were her outcry preserved in his memory that reappeared as a late echo from unknown depths at a certain place of his memories, unrecognized as repetition of the words mother had cried at the cemetary.

The other case concerns a woman in her late thirties who

was single and who was occupied as a social worker. She was connected with a coeducational grammar and high school and took care of several cases of boys and girls in the age-group from seven to seventeen. Shy and reserved, she functioned well in the profession she had chosen for herself. She lived with her mother with whom she could not get along because mother criticized her constantly. She asserted that mother, as far as she could remember, had never given her any affection, but had concentrated all attention and love on the patient's brother, John, who was three years younger than she. A certain scene from her childhood returned in her memories: she and John sat on the ground and at the mother's feet. The mother caressed John, but not the little girl. This representative memory was important because it dates a change in the attitude of the girl towards her mother who, she asserted, showed never the slightest expression of love for her.

The patient spoke once of the different attitude boys and girls had towards her and her social work. Girls in general liked to come to her and to consult her, asked for appointments while boys in general were unwilling to come to her consultation and were defiant. There are, she said, certainly exceptions. She discussed in great detail the case of an adolescent girl of whom she had to take care professionally. This pupil consistently showed a front of rebelliousness and defiance and seemed to reject all attempts of the social worker to win her confidence. She seemed to care for no one and not to mind that teachers and classmates did not pay attention to her. The social worker, my patient, characterized the attitude of this refractory girl as amounting to saying to all people, "Go to hell!" The patient recognized that the girl concealed a gentle and soft inclination behind that obstinate and rejecting attitude and she felt very sorry for her. This feeling increased in intensity when she was told that the mother of the girl was a hard and anti-demonstrative woman who had not given affection to the daughter in her childhood. Once the patient only with great effort controlled an impulse to put her hand in a caress on the head of the girl and to pacify and to reassure her with nice words. In this scene there came to the surface, unknown to the patient, a memory from her own childhood which was acted out. The girl whom she had asked, "Don't you think that I like you?" and who had answered, "I don't give a damn if you like me or not" must have unconsciously reminded her of her own defiant attitude as a child towards her mother, when she was the age that girl is now in. In the scene she described she has taken over the part of mother and the girl represented herself. This acting out contradicts thus her conscious thought that mother never showed affection to her and brings on a detour back the unconscious memory that she defiantly rejected any tender approach of mother to her. The significance of this psychoanalytic reconstruction of a forgotten piece of the past was proved in the later period of her analytic treatment.

Patients sometimes tell us small incidents from early years which, if considered as such, appear almost meaningless if we do not succeed in excavating the emotions that are not there. When those lost feelings are found, the memories cast a new light on the character of the patient when he was a child. Here is a representative example of this kind: a six-year-old boy, playing ball with other boys, once behaved strangely when one of his playmates fell down and hurt himself. While the other children occupied themselves helping and consoling their playmate, the boy ran away from the playground as if haunted and went directly home. Thirty years later while the man was in psychoanalytic treatment the memory of this little scene emerged amongst other reminiscences and puzzled the patient as much as me, his psychoanalyst. A few days later he remembered another scene preceding the accident in the playground. When he was four years old, he had once pushed his younger brother down the stairs. The knee of the little boy had been hurt and the parents had severely punished and reproached the malefactor. His strange behavior on the playground is explainable by the memory of this previous scene. He took to flight on an occasion that unconsciously reminded him of the earlier incident. No trail stays covered, when psychoanalytically explored.

PART TEN

Paradoxes and Patterns

---

1. THE PATH

For the man the path of greatest advantage is in most cases preferable to the path of least resistance. For the woman the path of greatest sexual resistance is often identical with the path of greatest advantage.

2. HIS WIFE

Heinrich Heine's wife Mathilde who was a French midinette could not speak German. She picked up a few expressions from the conversations of the poet with German friends, including the words *"Meine Frau."* She called herself thus. I am suspicious of the many biographers who consider such funny use as signs of Mathilde's naïvité. I rather think that in saying *"Meine Frau"* the woman expressed a cheerful mixture of pride and possessive devotion. Many women thinking of themselves in relation to their husbands are close to calling themselves in their thoughts *"seine Frau."*

3. DOWRY IN EUROPE

In many circles of Europe girls at their marriage were bestowed with a dowry. Consciously or unconsciously women consider the beautiful qualities of their bodies part of their dowry with which God or Mother Nature endowed them. Many brides look at themselves before the wedding night and ask themselves if their husbands will be satisfied with this dowry.

In an old cartoon of the German magazine *Simplicissimus* a worried father discussing with his wife their daughter who is still single says, "It is a pity that the girl has no dowry. If she had at least a beautiful bosom an idealist might be found."

4. SEARCH FOR THE MAN

The admonition *"Cherchez la femme"* is certainly to a great extent justified in the motivation of crimes and in very few other directions. It is for instance rare that the plan of a new scientific or artistic project can be traced back to the inspiration of a woman or to the infatuation of the researcher or artist with a girl. It is much more likely that a woman who for instance becomes suddenly interested in the construction of bridges has probably made the acquaintance of an engineer. When she meets a man interested in politics she may suddenly show enthusiasm for a certain political party or idea. As a matter of psychological fact, the saying *"Cherchez l'homme"* would be much more appropriate than the other one.

5. MYTHOLOGICAL FIGURES

Whoever conjured up the idea of justice personified by woman? This bit of Roman mythology is surely a misfit or a hoax! Other Roman personifications such as Pietas, Fecunditas and Pax can well be seen as female characters. At least, they do not contradict the concept of femininity. But Justitia? Think only of the symbolical attributes of that figure as she appears on numerous monuments. She holds a pair of scales as symbol of weighing right and wrong. But, since when have we conceived of woman as forming fair judgments about people, balancing the pros and cons? The sword the goddess of Justitia carries is certainly a masculine attribute. The blindfold before the figure's eyes indicating that justice judges without distinction or respect of persons, is an especially inappropriate attribute of the female character. A woman in this situation would surely peek from behind the blindfold to see the person upon whom she will deliver sentence.

6. Paradoxical Behavior Patterns

A widow who was wooed by a younger man to whom she was very attracted, sometimes caught herself wishing he would leave in the middle•of his visits. It became clear in psychoanalytical sessions that at those times she became afraid he would find out that she was not very well educated and often could not follow his abstract train of thoughts. Another patient who reached full vaginal orgasm in sexual intercourse with her husband, insists that she doesn't really like him, finds fault with some mannerisms of his speech and so on. She is also reticent about caressing him or responding to his expressions of love—she shows a behavior comparable to that of a certain lady described by Karl Kraus, who said, "To sleep with him, yes, but no intimacies please!" It finally became clear during psychoanalysis that the patient was always afraid that if she should show a man she loved him, he would consider her inferior and would leave her.

7. The Imprint of Personality

Goethe said, "In order to create something, one has to be someone." He meant the man's work reflects his personality. How is this with woman and her task? My mother used to say: "Every cow can *become* a mother." That is so, but no cow can be a mother, that means educate a child. His education is the very task of motherhood. Her personality will be reflected in the result of upbringing and educating the child as that of the man in his work.

8. Calling His Bluff

In the good old days a traveling salesman making a trip to Italy sent a night letter to his wife in Vienna:

> If I were a bird
> I would fly home, dear,
> Since I can't fly
> I make love here.

Her answer said:

> I don't believe a word
> Of your wire from Rome.
> You can do it as little there
> As you can do it at home.

9. Promiscuity and Romance

It is almost a platitude to state that women who are promiscuous must have a low opinion of themselves. It should be added that such women usually step aside and avoid competition with the majority of their sex. In living promiscuously they preconsciously confess: we are whores and unable to compete with women who have a great deal of self-esteem. Individual analysis will decide whether such avoidance is founded on unconscious homosexual tendencies or on unconsciously perceived ideas of their unworthiness. It is likely that a combination of both factors is operating.

10. MATERIAL

A bachelor I know had rented a part of an apartment and furnished it himself. His landlady had undertaken to dust and clean his rooms. In a very short while she made a nuisance of herself by nagging the tenant daily about his carelessness and negligence towards the furniture. He took this for some time and then one day exploded, "But it's my furniture after all! I can destroy it all if I want to!" To his surprise this made absolutely no impression on her. She continued to nag him and to regard the furniture as though it were hers or as if she had adopted it. He attributed the care with which she treated it to some mysterious feminine characteristic connected with a tendency to put away "for yourselves treasures upon earth where moth and rust doth corrupt" (St. Mathew VI 19). But he did not consider the fact that women so to speak "instinctively" treat pieces of furniture as if they were parts of their own body and that they unconsciously conceive of damages and injuries done to them as of physical harm inflicted upon them.

11. THE PERSONAL

The separation of the personal and subjective side from the objective and factual in an issue is under certain circumstances difficult for the man. Here is, however, no problem for the woman because it does not even occur to her to try to separate the personal from the objective side.

The past is not dear to them as such. Anniversaries are only occasions to revivify old emotional experiences. They need no reconstruction of the past because it was never buried. Nor do they need any magic flying carpets to transport them to places in which they once were and which they liked. The rug in their dining room is a sufficient reminder to bring back the place in which they were once happy. As they transform the past into the present, they re-experience the sight, the sound and the fragrance of remote places without leaving the couch upon which they daydream. Yes, women live for the Now and Here, but this moment and this place can include the remotest past and the most distant places.

12. Loving Oneself

It seems that it is easier for the woman than for the man to regress from a state of disappointed love to loving herself. In analytic terms, from object-love to narcissism. A woman who feels bitter about not getting a gift from a loved person will buy herself a present. Purchasing a new hat will console her about the missed sign of being loved by another. She can love herself so to speak vicarously in the absence of her lover, but also in anticipation of him. It seems that self-love is for her much more than for man a necessary condition for becoming ready to love and for being loved.

13. The In-Laws

During the World War II the magazine *Stars and Stripes* offered a prize for the best answer to the question of how

Hitler, that arch-enemy of mankind, should be punished. The answers suggested various tortures and punishments. The prize was won by a Jewish soldier of the American division in Italy who suggested, "He should live with my in-laws in the Bronx."

A young woman, thinking of marriage, rarely anticipates the character of her future fathe -in-law, but she hardly ever forgets that she will have a mother-in-law. The psychological importance of her figure was well defined by someone who said "The mother of a son is the destiny of her future daughter-in-law."

14. Never Underestimate the Power of Women

According to Homer's Odyssey the sorceress Circe could transform men into swine. Any beautiful enchantress of today can do this and can do even more, for instance make a monkey of a man.

A pessimistic view of the future of mankind will point to the fact that man is fanatical and does not hesitate to destroy those who have different opinions in social, religious or national questions. At the moment men are divided into two camps: they threaten each other with annihilation because they have contrary views about how mankind can be made happy. The hope of the world rests on women. Fanaticism of this kind is alien to them. They know that hate based on whatever reasons cannot make man happier, not even the hater himself. Only love can perform this miracle.

15. Permanence

There is a question whether the immanent wish for permanence in love relationships, so regularly experienced by women does not have a biological prototype. Such a primal model would determine all later processes and could claim a pattern-forming significance. I mean the tendency to keep the embryo within the woman, to retain it as long as possible. The separation from mother is then made possible only by the catastrophe of birth.

Even a continuation of this biological speculation would be imaginable: a woman who wants to make a home and cook for her husband fulfills perhaps a function anticipating another much more vital one; namely to prepare a comfortable place for her baby in the womb and to store up nourishment for it within herself. While taking care of the man, she without knowing it anticipates her future role of mother. She serves the interests of the species while she believes she is only a good wife and housekeeper.

16. PLAYING WITH FIRE

A woman who is flirting is often not aware that she is playing with fire. She is not endangered as long as her attention is concentrated on the experiment of testing her desirability on a certain man. But sometimes a spark of the fire she wants to inflame the man with leaps over to herself. Such cases belong to the realm of occupational hazards.

17. WINNING HER OVER

It is well known that the situation during an analytic session is characterized by the fact that the patient lays relaxed on the couch while the analyst sits unseen behind him or her. I once ran into unexpected resistance of a woman-patient when I tried to point out the reasons for this special position in the beginning of her analytic treatment. She refused to accept my explanations until I said, "You see, when you sit on this chair across me, I have an unfair advantage over you. I look at a young and beautiful girl and you look at an old, bald man."

18. Mate Choice

The problem of the mate choice is still unsolved in spite of the numerous attempts undertaken to explain the special attraction one person has for another person of the opposite sex. Since Goethe in his "Elective Affinities" expressed the guess that incentives, comparable to those operating in chemical processes, are working between the involved persons, biologists and psychologists tried to find the laws governing the seemingly irrational choice of a mate. It seems until now that psychoanalysis is unable to make a contribution to the solution of this problem. Clinical studies have perhaps a better chance if they would take a different point of departure. In psychoanalysis the therapist sometimes gets the impression that a kind of unconscious purposefulness determines the mismatings of couples in such a way that the neurotic symptoms and inhibitions of one partner complements those of the other. For many married couples sexual intercourse is an exchange of failures. They are, as the French say, "mauvais coucheurs."

19. Secret Affair

It is not too difficult to conceal an extramarital relationship between a man and a woman as long as they are not observed together. A man will be able to keep the secret of an affair with a married woman when he is discreet and especially when he does not mix in the same social circle. It is much more difficult to keep such a relationship secret when both man and woman are part of the same company. Women especially are very sensitive and perceptive in this direction. They can guess a hidden sexual affair much sooner than men, who often do not have any notion of its existence. It seems that women have in general better antennae for human relations than men.

20. ASHAMED OF MOTHER

A patient remembers from his childhood the first time he was ashamed of his mother before his playmates. He was playing marbles at the corner near his home in the lower East Side of New York. Mother called down from the fourth floor kitchen window, "Joe, come for your milk!" He felt as if he had been treated like a baby before the other boys. A little girl of the same age would have reacted differently on this occasion. She too could feel ashamed of her mother, but under different circumstances.

21. INTOLERANCE TO IRONY

Paranoid persons can stand direct criticism much better than sarcasm, irony or critical allusions because they suspect the person speaking is still hiding stronger objections and reproaches. Similarly women and children are intolerant to irony and allusions because they entertain the same suspicions. The common feature between these groups is their inner insecurity.

22. The Hidden Significance

A man had a regrettable accident which developed into an emotional crisis with his wife. The unfortunate husband praised the dress a certain woman was wearing at a party without remembering that he had spoken rather critically of a quite similar dress his own wife had bought a short while ago. In the ensuing stormy scene the wife heaped abuses on him. Her psychological mistake was that her remarks were concentrated on the dress. In reality the man was not interested in the dress that the other woman wore, but in the lady herself or rather in her body, its curves, her legs and thighs and so on. His observations were a clumsy attempt at displacement of his sexual interest and the dress appeared only as a cover—literally and metaphorically—of the sexual attraction exerted by this other woman. He was searching for the figure underneath the dress.

23. Individuality

Differentiation and individualization is more widespread in men than in women. Women mold themselves and identify themselves more readily with their love-objects. They might admire individuality in men, but they do not like the aloneness and loneliness connected with it. They will never agree with Ibsen's saying that the strong ones are more powerful when alone. They are much more sociable than men. Nature has prepared them with their future role of wife and mother much more than she has men for their part as husbands and fathers which is rather a role men have to improvise when they become head of a family.

24. Hurricanes in America

Hurricanes are properly called women's names in America. The comparison with women's emotional outbreaks fails only because women's moods are rarely so destructive as the outbreaks of nature.

25. Frustration

A woman patient had many complaints about her husband and presented herself as the poor and helpless victim of his moods. During the analytic treatment it became clear that the woman was a headstrong and domineering person while the husband appeared as a weak and gentle man who yielded to her wishes except in some decisions which, it is true, concerned the most important issues of their common life. In these he gently, but firmly stood his ground. Once an actual event of vital impact made it necessary that the husband consult me. He also spoke of his relationship with his wife. He said, "It was clear to me soon after the wedding that my wife wanted to make me a henpecked husband. She became frustrated through my yielding to her." The man had characterized the situation very well: if he had resisted her and fought with her she would perhaps have succeeded in bringing him under her thumb. He frustrated her efforts by giving in on all unimportant decisions while he remained adamant on the great questions of their marital life.

26. Sleeping Beauty

Fairy tales tell a lot about sexual secrets. The story of the Sleeping Beauty presents a striking metaphor for the sexual awakening of the young girl when she is kissed by a man. Fairy tales do not tell everything, of course. We can, for instance, assume that the Sleeping Beauty was not altogether asleep when the prince approached her, but observed his coming through half-closed eyes while she pretended to be asleep.

27. CHOICE

Dialogue before dinner: "What kind of fruit would you like—stewed prunes or apple sauce?" The man, "Whatever you like." "But I asked what *you* like?" "It's the same to me." From such a beginning a tiff often develops. Psychologically viewed, the man gave the wrong answer. Insensitive and imperceptive as men are, he did not answer as the woman had expected or hoped he would. She had wanted to hear praise, or at least acknowledgment of the fact that she had prepared both kinds of fruit for him, and that she was concerned about what he liked. His answer was indifferent, which means psychologically wrong.

28. SEXUAL MORALS AND THE LAW

What two adult, mentally sane persons in possession of the full power of their will, do with each other sexually, is their own affair and does not concen anybody, certainly not the government. In this sense there is no such thing as a separate sexual morality nor such a thing as a separate and definite sexual crime. That which is called by this name is generally an offense against persons who are legally under age or otherwise unable to have a will of their own or an insult or injury inflicted on immature persons, in connection with sexuality. When such offences are legally indicted, it should be done with the point of view valid for crimes of theft, robbery and assault. The state is in no way entitled to forbid any kind of sexual performances except in cases of violence, illegal detention and so on. Otherwise the lawgivers assume an authority to which they are not entitled. Everybody wants to get into the sexual act.

29. OBSERVATION

I wonder if psychologists ever make experiments to determine the differences in the kind and scope of observation of the sexes. Such experiments, made in various fields of observation, for instance at a social party or at a college lecture and with men and women of the same age and similar education, would cast a surprising light not only on the selectivity of attention of both sexes, but also on the differences in the subjects of this attention and observation by men and women. It would for instance result in the decision that women are in general better observers and more perceptive in many directions than men, but that their observations are more influenced by emotional factors while their psychological interpretations of the observed subjects are generally closer to the truth than those of men.

30. MASOCHISM

The simplest and most elementary pattern of masochism is the enjoyable misery of a woman who wears beautiful, but too small shoes. There is a proverb, "Vanity has to suffer." It is often applied to women who have to undergo painful sensations in beauty-salons. The feminine character of masochism becomes transparent when you turn the sentence around. Suffering appears then as motivated or accompanied by satisfaction of vanity.

31. CURIOSITY

They say that curiosity killed the cat, but they forget to add that curiosity kept so many other cats alive. Gossiping is the other side of women's occupation with human concern, it is, so to speak, the other side of a valuable coin.

32. DEATH

The idea of death has often another character for women than for men and is not as frequently connected in their thoughts with punishment for sins. In Schubert's song Death says to the maid, "I don't come to punish thee," and in Richard Strauss' opera death approaches Ariadne as the beautiful God of Love.

33. PRIDE

Pride is the greatest vice of man. If he had a lower basic opinion of human nature, he would be more humble and more ready to accept himself. The unconscious idea of grandeur living in man makes him intolerant towards his own weaknesses and shortcomings and to those of others. This severity and intolerance propels him in the last consequences to become cruel and vicious. He often thinks of himself as especially bad—which is an attitude just as grandiose and conceited as the opposite one. He is nothing special: much lower than the angels and not much higher than the beasts. Women are in this direction more tolerant towards themselves and others. They don't treat themselves so harshly nor do they feel such a hate against the weaknesses and short-comings of others that they have to burn them on a stake or put them in gas-chambers for divergent beliefs.

34. Fun

The expression "to have fun" becomes in America more and more synonymous with having sexual intercourse. This new connotation is symptomatical of the emotional degradation of the sexual process. Sexual experience is in reality very serious, and sometimes even tragic. If it's only fun, it is not even funny any longer.

35. Adaptability

Women, not yet set in their ways, can be molded by life and can adapt themselves so much easier to changed circumstances and surroundings. They can take over their husband's nationality and religions with the same ease as his name. Vagueness and indefiniteness allow them to become almost anything in contrast to man who is much more rigid and less adaptable.

36. Education

We are proud that boys and girls are educated in our schools in the same way, learn the same things and study the same disciplines. Yet it is psychologically obvious that the same material of the study has not the identical meaning for the male and female student. If it were possible to penetrate to the core of the mind, even numbers mean something different to men and women and an equation has one personal face and significance for a girl and another for a boy.

37. Metaphor and Psychosomatic Complaint

A woman patient complained about "piercing sensations" in the heart. No organic cause for the symptom was found. Psychoanalysis could recognize that those very unpleasant sensations emerged whenever the patient did or said something of which her mother, who had died many years ago, would have disapproved. When the patient was a little girl and in her early teens, she often heard mother say, "It is as if you stab me in the heart" whenever the daughter's behavior gave cause for reproach. The unconscious memory of this sentence explains the character of the complaint.

PART ELEVEN

At All Ages

1. THE BOY IN THE MAN

Was it accidental that, on the same day, two quotations of great men came my way—both envisaging the child in the man? Friedrich Nietzsche speaks to women, "In the man there is hidden a child who wants to play. Get up then, you women, and wake me the child in the man!" Here is the self-characterization of one of the greatest scientists, Sir Isaac Newton, "I do not know what I may appear to the world, but in myself I seem to have been only like a boy playing on the seashore and diverting myself in the now and then, finding a smoother pebble and a prettier shell than ordinary, whilst the great ocean of truth lay all undiscovered before me."

It is only a comparison, but is this kind of comparison accidental? Is it only fanciful and fortuituous? The most feminine among women have long ago intuitively understood that there is a boy hidden in every man, a child who wants to play. Such a concept need not stop them from taking man's play seriously, knowing that, to him, it is the most important thing in his life. But also a little boy considers his play the center of his existence. On the other side tolerance for this compulsion to play is shown by maternal women. The Countess Tolstoy, whose husband was thought of as the greatest writer of his time, showed this attitude when she wrote in a letter about the social reform projects of her famous mate, developed when he was already an old man. "It does not matter what the child likes to try. The main thing is that he should not cry."

2. THE OUTSIDERS

Through psychoanalysis we became acquainted with a kind of foreknowledge about the sexuality living in little boys and girls long before they were told the facts of life. Children form, at this time, various infantile sexual theories—a mixture of grotesque or mistaken ideas intermingled with some quite correct deductions—about the sexual activity of adults. You will rarely find in psychoanalytical literature descriptions of the astonishment experienced by children who are first confronted with the phenomenon of adult sexuality. Rarely are the feelings described of the fact that these children sense that they are excluded or outside the circle of the dance of life. Little boys especially, at a certain phase of their life, seem to feel that all grown-ups are continually occupied or preoccupied by sexuality. This view sometimes leads to an impression of a kind of frenzy and incomprehensible passion in their environment and to a burning desire of the boy to be included in the sexual round-dance.

The counterpart to this view and attitude of astonishment and amazement at the general sexual interest is to be found in old age. Old men are often so remote from the experiences of their own youth that they look at the sexual activities of young people with great surprise. The Austrians used to tell a story about their Kaiser Franz who died in 1835. The emperor once took (on a hot summer night), a walk with his adjutant in the Park of Schoenbrunn, near the royal castle in Vienna. The Kaiser, then a very old man, and his accompanying officer surprised a young couple copulating. The emperor turned to his adjutant and asked, astonished, "Do people still do that?"

3. WOMAN'S RELATIONS WITH MOTHER

If a woman is not reconciled with her mother, she will never get along with men. To be internally reconciled does not mean that she must love her mother. Not even the Holy Scripture prescribes that one should love one's parents, only that one should honor them. Love cannot be ordered. Inner reconciliation means that a daughter will think of, or look at her mother with feelings of understanding or empathy, or with the recognition that her mother has done the best she knew how to do in a difficult life. This insight that a woman must be reconciled with her mother, has been recognized by most analysts independently, although perhaps it is formulated here for the first time clearly. We cannot definitely state why this has to be so; however, we can point out that the woman transfers to her relation with men, her early love for mother and we take into consideration the pattern-forming significance of this first love of childhood. This reconciliation with mother facilitates woman's later identification with mother. There is another factor best illustrated by a story I heard the other day. A mother and her little daughter, visiting the New York zoo, came to the cage of a lioness who was giving birth to a cub. The attendant of the zoo tried to remove the people from the sight. However, he was not in time and the child witnessed the delivery of the cub. She heard the groans of pain of the lioness and remained transfixed. When it was over, she walked in silence beside her mother for a while. At the exit of the park, the little girl suddenly bent over and, taking her mother's hand, kissed it.

4. Time, Place and the Sexes

Men think that women live in the present, for the moment and for the little place in which they live. Some psychologists have expressed the view that women have no historic sense and their existence is tied to, and concentrated on, the Here and Now. But how is this alleged deficiency brought in harmony with the well known fact that women never forget anniversaries, birthdays and other data important in their life and in the lives of those near and dear to them? Granted they live for the present, but the past is not dead for them but can become present at a moment. They do not seem to feel that never-ceasing curiosity a man has to know about foreign countries, and they show little desire to discover the mysteries of the stratosphere.

The seeming contradiction can be solved with a little psychological insight. When women remember anniversaries, it is not the date they wish to recall, but the emotional situation. They reexperience the feelings they had at their wedding. They live again the joy felt at the first sight of their baby. It is not important to them that their husbands should remember the historical date of the wedding day or of their first meeting. What is essential is that their husband should maintain the same love for them as then. Not the actual history, but the loyalty and love shown to them are significant for them. Not the remembrance itself, but the permanence of feeling is what makes those dates essential. They feel hurt when their lovers or husbands let such a significant anniversary pass unnoticed. They feel that this means a loss of the feelings accompanying those events. Their sense of history is not a scientific or academic interest.

5. Transformation by Love

Love has a different psychological meaning for women than it has for men. This difference starts with the divergence of connotation of the very word and reaches to the area of its emotional significance for the two sexes. In spite of its impact and importance in the life of a man, it generally cannot form the center of his life. He can lose control for minutes, or even for hours through love, but it does not transform his personality to the same extent and in the same depth as it does a woman's. In women, their body as well as their soul goes through a metamorphosis under the influence of love. I have seen fat women lose weight when in love, ugly ones become beautiful. In short, woman often acquires a new personality in love. She can become another woman—altogether different from what she had been before. She sometimes sheds her old skin and acquires a new one like a serpent. . . . She is herself frequently astonished by the depth and scope of the transformation brought about by the new sensation, as though it were a miracle. She belonged to herself before and she does not any longer. Before she met the man, she at least knew she was herself. Now she has taken him within herself and her life is his as well as hers. No man appears to feel any such deep change within himself. Also in this direction, in the emotional incorporation of the love-object woman's love is a prelude to becoming pregnant, which is, properly seen, a transformation of her organism through the absorption of a foreign body.

6. Skirts

Men's pants are simply a part of their clothing and nothing else. A woman's skirt is that too, but it is also almost a part of her body expressed in the form of material and clothing. What you can do with pants is very simple: you can put them on or take them off. The uses of a skirt are many and manifold. A patient (who was not a voyeur) described to me what a woman he often observed did with her skirt. The patient never saw the woman's face nor her whole body. He lived across the street from her and the position of the apartment was such that he could only see the lower part of her figure—and this only during the day as the blinds were pulled down in the evening. The patient described the movements of the skirt as though it were a living thing. As a matter of fact he described it as "a part of a woman disguised as a garment." He observed the unknown woman both when she was alone and when she was in company. He felt that both pulling the skirt up a little and tucking it down could be a form of flirtation—attracting the man's attention and arousing his interest in her body. The skirts the woman wore, he asserted, reflected her moods and were not determined only by social occasions. They switched and whirled, danced, felt gay or tired and sad. . . . Here is an instance of the personification of a skirt from a mystery novel by Agatha Christie; "Her skirts were tweedy and had a depressed droop at the back."

The imagination of the patient exaggerated the expressions he attributed to the woman's skirts. Yet there is no doubt that woman expresses her moods in their shape, color and movement more than a man does in his trousers. Her skirt seems not only to cover her body but to play around it, both concealing and revealing it. How plastic is, for instance, the image of a canteen girl in love with a soldier marching off with his regiment, in a song of Johannes Brahms, *"Sie nimmt ihre Röcke zusammen und läuft dem Reiter nach."* ("She pulls her skirts together and runs after the rider.")

The other day a line came back to me:

> I, for one, venerate a petticoat,
> A garment of mystical sublimity,
> No matter whether russet, silk or dimity.

By whom is that? By Byron.* I must have been reminded of the line when I saw a woman raise her skirts a little when she stepped into a car. For a moment, I wondered what dimity was . . . . some material for clothes? I dismissed the thought. But later I resumed it, I thought: How old does one get! Who, today, conceives of a petticoat as a garment of mystical sublimity? For whom are short skirts still a subject of sexual excitement? I still remember having laughed as a boy at a cartoon in which Charlie sees his aunt bicycling and shouts highly astonished, "Look! Auntie, too, has legs!" Now, looking at that cartoon and its caption you and I would ask, "What is funny about that?"

7. Aspects of Feminine Shame

When I was in my late teens the following incident occurred. A group of boys and girls made an excursion on horseback up a high mountain near Vienna. When they arrived at the peak and entered the hotel they heard that there was to be a dance for the guests. Eager to take part in the pleasure, the girls decided to borrow skirts from the waitresses as, in those times, it would have been incongruous

* *Don Juan*, C. XIV, XXVI.

to dance in riding breeches. They simply put the skirts on over their boots and pants and enjoyed the dance. During the intermissions they all went into the bar and drank some wine. Stimulated by the wine, the young men suggested that the girls raise their skirts. All the girls rejected the idea as highly indecent although they were fully dressed underneath in their riding breeches and boots. The fact that they were fully dressed was of no importance. The lasciviousness was implied in the gesture.

It is very possible for a woman to experience shame before the man with whom she has just slept. Although he has seen her in the nude, she may very well say to him, "Turn around while I dress." This can easily be understood in psychological terms. The man who was blinded by desire is now sober and aware. He may not look at her with the same eyes, but critically.

There are sometimes moments, even in the midst of sexual surrender of the woman, when she might be flushed with sudden shame, overcome by attacks of *"sudaine pudeur."*

A young woman in one of Georges Simenon's recent detective novels explains to Inspector Maigret why she thought she could get a job in a department-store as a salesgirl: women who purchase underwear and girdles don't like to be served by a male clerk.

Apropos being served by men and women: in beauty salons so called "shampoo-girls" wash and rinse the women's hair, but men set it. Why should the girls do only the "dirty work," namely the washing and cleaning and men should have the artistic part of the operation? Is it because Mr. Carlos or Mr. Caruso can better judge which kind of coiffure is becoming in the case of this or that customer? Do women trust the taste of a man more than that of another woman with regard to the hair-do? It is even possible that there is a resistance in women themselves against this task. One of them, asked about it, said, "Why should I do my best to make another woman more beautiful?" And why is it usually men who serve women in shoe stores? Do men develop more patience with the ladies who are very choosy in buying shoes? Or is it because most men are latently shoe-fetichists? Someone asserted that women do not like to kneel before other women who try shoes on. Well, if it's not kneeling, it is some lower position which comes close to kneeling. All those questions are not only to be seen from commercial points of view, but also from those of comparative psychology. Yes even some sexual symbolism for instance in trying shoes on a woman plays a decisive role. (Think of the Cinderella-story.)

8. THE SENSE OF BEAUTY

According to psychoanalytic theory the little girl discovers early in life, by the observation of boys, that the other sex is privileged in having external genitals, while she has none. This startling discovery leaves ineradicable traces in her development and character formation. It is at the root of the greater narcissistic attitude which psychoanalysis attributes to women. Their vanity was defined by Helene Deutsch as a further effect of penis-envy, "for they are driven to rate their physical charms more highly as a belated compensation for their original sexual inferiority."*

It seems to me that psychoanalytic research in emphasizing the physical deficiency in the genitals-region which the little girl experiences, has neglected the esthetic value and its

* "The Psychology of Women in Relation to the Function of Reproduction," *International Journal of Psychoanalysis*, 1925, p. 160.

significance in the development of the feminine attitude. I assume that the little girl who compares her genitals to those of the little boy, finds her own ugly. Not only the greater modesty of women, but their never ceasing striving toward beautifying and adoring their bodies is to be understood as displacement and extension of their effort to overcompensate for their original impression that their genitals were ugly. So many characteristics of women have to be conceived as manifestations of this wish to be beautiful, often transferred from their body to their apparel, their dresses, their jewels and so on. We have thus to thank the vivid sense of beauty and the better taste women possess to an initial shocking impression of their childhood in which they considered themselves handicapped, inferior and ugly compared with the boys.

It is not only the genital differences perceived by the little girl which make her feel at a disadvantage and promote her penis-envy. One of the reasons rarely discussed is the training in feminine daintiness in connection with her genitals. Education leads the little girl to the idea that her glands secrete unpleasant odors. The majority of women are panicky at the thought that a man might notice some vaginal smell. Deep within her, a woman fears that all the perfumes of Arabia will not sweeten the secretions of her genitals. Nothing similar appears in the education of the boy. He pays little attention to his own secretions. No man is concerned with the odor of his genitals before sexual intercourse and every woman is.

9. COUNTERPARTS IN EMOTIONAL DISTURBANCES

Although psychotic and prepsychotic disturbances show superficially the same picture with both sexes, finer observation can recognize differences even in their symptomatology. Compare the two cases of paranoia of the erotomanic kind, met with a man and with a woman. The man who consulted me complained that all men whom he sees are out to attract his attention and want to "make him." To convince me of the truth of his statement, he took me to the window of my consultation room, (at that time on the sixth floor) and pointed to the passers-by on the street. "Do you see that man there below? Did you observe how he straightened his tie when he saw me? And that other one—did you see that he waved at me while he pretended to greet an acquaintance?" In this way he interpreted little gestures of passing men as intended to attract his attention. A middle-aged woman complained that another woman who lived across the street always watched her and observed her when she dressed and undressed, and peeked at her in the evening through Venetian blinds because she was in love with her. Both paranoic patients unconsciously reject their homosexual trends in projecting them to objects, but the male patient shows more energy of sexual desire.

10. SUPEREGO—DEVELOPMENT OF THE SEXES

The superego is, so to speak, the monument of the commanding and forbidding father within the individual who has replaced the actual father-figure by an invisible agency within his ego. It seems that the superego of the woman does not develop the rigidity and severity of that of the man because the sexual and aggressive drives in her are not so intensive as to necessitate the rigorous counterforces in their control. It is perhaps therefore that she does not evolve such severe discipline in self-denial and need not refrain from pleasures and comforts. Her more gentle ego does not often force her into asceticisms in religion and in everyday life.

There is also no masochistic system comparable to that of the man. A scientist I knew adhered to such a pervasive system. Varying the title of the Shakespeare's play he called that rule of conduct "Pleasure for Pleasure." That meant that when he was preoccupied with research and enjoyed the satisfaction of discovery, he had to deny himself the pleasure of theater or music. When he indulged in sport, he could not allow himself to enjoy female company and so on. It is, of course, possible that women do without things they enjoy and are willing to forego a pleasure for another gratification, but their trading is never so rigid and unconditional nor so pervasive. They are in general too reasonable to form such a severe code. They keep a diet to have a good figure and suffer in beauty parlors to improve their appearance. They are willing and able—sometimes more than men—to make severe sacrifices for the sake of loved persons, but never or hardly ever for a cause or an impersonal task. There is no god who witnesses their self-denials nor do they sacrifice their pleasure to an exacting deity. They don't mean to please Yahweh, but a man, or many men. Even monotheism is an invention of man. No woman would arrive at the idea that there is only one god.

11. Older Women, Older Men

In a bar in lower Manhattan is a board on which the following advice is inscribed:

> Always take a woman past forty
> They don't tell
> They don't swell
> And they are grateful as hell

It is not advisable to ask older ladies how their health is because you run the risk that they will tell you all their complaints with full details.

Someone asserted that a man gets tired of his honesty after his fortieth year and a woman of her chastity. Are honesty and chastity thus imperiled in our society? By no means; it is only that the temptations to transgress at this age become stronger or the inhibitions weaker. It is true that after forty the danger in both directions is greater. However, the concepts of honesty and chastity are not consciously devaluated at this age; at least not officially because it is the age in which men have become fathers who teach their sons honesty and women mothers who educate their daughters to remain chaste. Thus although those fathers and mothers transgress the codes of society its values are ascertained and preserved by transmission to and education of the young generation.

Enjoyment of life is intimately connected with the capability to do stupid things. Only illusions give content and color to life. Goethe said: "When you are stirred up in heart and mind, what better things do you want? Who cannot err nor cannot love any longer, should let himself be buried." Madame de Stael's sentence should be changed "Tout comprendre c'est tout renoncer."

Young men hope in general that their situation will change for the better. A decisive point in life is reached when men, now old, express the hope that all will remain as it is and will not change for the worse. A character in Paul Claude's play *The Hostage* remarks that he is not guided by the light of the spirit, but by the much weaker light of conscience. With very few exceptions, among whom I count Schweitzer and

Churchill, most old men are led by this weaker light. The erosion of values in old age operates in this direction even with men of genius.

Men who are unwilling to accept middle age are feminine. Women who easily accept theirs are masculine.

The malicious pages at the court of Louis XIV opening a door for ladies used to say *"Passez, Beauté!"* When the woman has gone through the door, they sometimes added: *"Beauté passée."* Women sometimes pity old men they see in the park sitting alone; men rarely feel sorry for old women. Old men are more helpless and lonely. Their life in old age loses more and more the content that only human relations can provide. Old women can enjoy life with their children and grandchildren and in the company of other women.

12. IN THE LAND OF SMILES

The title of Lehar's operetta, *The Land of Smiles*, applied to China, is a very appropriate name for the area where women live. Think that the smile of a man expresses a very restricted amount of emotions while that of a woman runs the whole gamut of her true or pretended feelings. There are frozen smiles and smiles that melt the icy atmosphere between people. The time and occasion for feminine smiles is also subjected to fashions and conventions.

Almost eighty years ago the Swiss writer Gottfried Keller published a collection of short stories, *Das Sinngedicht*, now almost forgotten. One of the stories presents a young scientist, Reinhard, whose attention is diverted from his studies when he reads an epigram written by a seventeenth century German poet, Friedrich von Logau.

Wie wollst du weisse Lilien zu weissen Rosen
  machen?
Küss eine weisse Galathee, sie wird errötend lachen.

How wilt thou change white lilies to roses red, the
  while?
Kiss some fair nymph until she blushes, and blushing
  brightly smiles.

The young scientist is very eager to perform the experiment, but it fails at first. He kisses a girl, she laughs, but does not blush, he kisses another who blushes, but does not smile. Only after some time he encounters a young lady with whom he brings the experiment to a satisfactory conclusion.

Let us daringly assume that a young scientist of our own time would be turned away from his attempts to manufacture a more powerful bomb long enough to destroy mankind by a curiosity similar to that of Dr. Reinhard. How would he fare? I am afraid his experiment would result in a complete flop. What girl would, in our age, blush at all? And what girl would graciously smile at a kiss? A kiss is today either merely an empty formality or a damned serious prelude to sexual intercourse. A gracious combination of blushing and smiling is now as obsolete as the kind of guns soldiers used when Friedrich von Logau wrote that epigram more than three hundred years ago.

A patient who is not a poet, but a physicist, told me a lovely fantasy he had as a young man. He had fallen in love with a beautiful young girl, but had been for a long time too shy to tell her about his feelings. Once he took her into his arms and kissed her. He asked her if she had known that he loved her. She did not answer and only looked up at him. On the same evening the young man wrote the following fantasy: "Before the Lord's throne one of His most beautiful angels appeared with a complaint. The angel told the Lord that someone had stolen her smile while she had slept and had dreamed a wonderful dream, now forgotten. 'Your smile was not stolen,' said the Lord, 'it was only borrowed. Look down there.' The Lord pointed to a certain place on earth, to the room in which I had just held this girl in my arms. A ray of sun had danced into the room when I asked her if she knew that I loved her. She remained silent, but there was suddenly a most wonderful smile around her mouth while she looked seriously into my eyes and I thought, 'Only an angel can smile this way.' "

13. PUNCTUALITY

Punctuality is a demand created by a severe super-ego. To be unpunctual is conceived by our unconscious as being rude and offensive. It is in this sense that the sentence of Louis XVI, "Punctuality is the politeness of kings," has to be understood. The king, who is free from the conventional commandments which bind his subjects, voluntarily subjects himself to the obligation to be on time. Is to be punctual also the politeness of queens? Certainly not to the same degree. The difference of sex is quite important here. We do not expect, as we do of men, that women be on time for a date or an appointment. A silent agreement exists according to which women are supposed to let men wait, while it would be considered uncouth for a man not to be on time in meeting a woman. No man expects his date to be earlier at a certain place and then to wait for him. It seems that it is a part of the unwritten laws of gallantry that the man be early at the expected meeting place. The pattern-forming significance of sexuality—the man being active and taking the initiative—expresses itself also in this bit of behavior. To be late—or at all events, later—than the man, is thus the privilege of women in all walks of life. Our colored maid, Gussie, never went to the door at the first ring if she knew it was the delivery man who had rung the bell. She declared, "You must let a man wait."

14. Objection to Praise

I drove with a husband and wife to a party. He was in his late forties, she in her middle thirties. He spoke of a movie they had seen the day before, and of the French feminine star, whose physical endowments he praised. He was especially enthusiastic about the lovely legs of the actress and described them in detail. I agreed with moderation that she had, indeed, beautiful legs. To our astonishment his wife objected vividly to our praising. She said, "I don't understand you men. What's so wonderful about a leg? It's just a part of a human body and no different from any other." She continued in this vein, expressing some contempt for the male's appreciation of this part of female beauty. I had but rarely heard a woman object to complimentary remarks about her own sex in this manner and began to wonder about it. Soon I realized that our conversation was, in more ways than one, tactless. First of all, no woman wishes to hear praise about another woman from the men in her company. But, besides and beyond that, the very nature of the praise had probably offended the pride of the lady who listened to them. It was restricted to a single part of the woman's body as though it were isolated and separated from her person. Nothing was said about the qualities of the woman as an actress and artist, and nothing about her personality. The wife felt hurt because the remarks had degraded all women, including herself, in viewing them in a representative individual as though they were cattle seen at an exhibition.

15. BECOMING A MOTHER

It is very likely that love often takes a different course for women than it does for men. It begins, as does that of men, with fantasies regressing to the first phase of dependence—to the mother who gave the child warmth, protection, shelter, and food. The unconscious fantasy of the woman thus regresses to the realm of early wishes, to be held and embraced, to be cuddled and taken care of. In these fantasies, the woman returns to her childhood. The man takes later in her fantasies the place her mother, the first love object, once had. Later on, this really eternal wish to be "mothered" is replaced by the wish to take over the role and become a mother herself. By way of identification, the woman now wants to have a child, to care for it and mother it, rather than to be a child herself. The transition from this beginning phase to the end-phase of fantasy is formed by the man. He is, so to speak, the bridge from one side to the other. He not only will give her the child she wants, but he himself will be the child upon whom she will, in the meantime, lavish her love.

It must be immanent motherliness that makes women kind to others, to men as well as to women and fills them with horror at the thought of destroying life and to kill. Lady Macbeth had no children.

A neurotic patient said when shortly after the delivery she held her baby in her arms, "This is the first time that I do not hate men."

16. THE SECOND BEST

The psychological contrast between the sexes comes to a clear impression in the different values they place on their appearance and attributes. Men want to be strong and vigorous; their ideal is Hercules. Women want to be beautiful; their ideal is Venus. From the viewpoint of their infantile attitudes, both sexes are striving during their later years to overcome an unconscious fear of their early childhood. The man tries to master the castration-fear that overshadowed his boyhood. The woman attempts to conquer the little girl's impression that she was handicapped, compared with the boy because she has no penis. Both sexes thus fight phantoms in later years which loomed in their early past and try to find consolations for imagined defects.

With regard to their psychological significance two events in the lives of men and women cannot be compared to any other in their impact. The most important event in the life of a man is the death of his father (later on of a father-representative figure). The most important event in the life of a woman is the birth of a child (especially of a son). Both events are fulfillments of old, repressed wishes of childhood.

Love is originally an attempt to regain the ideal state of being unconditionally accepted, that means of a complete narcissistic satisfaction. As such it is as impossible to regain as a return to the paradise from which we were expelled. That paradisiacal situation was once really there, namely during early infancy. What we unconsciously wish in love is to re-experience our mother's first delight in us when we were babies, that means to regain paradise lost.

17. Avoidance of Incestuous Dangers

There are several ways of avoiding coming even close to the frontiers of incestuous desires. One way is the choice of a partner who is as concerns nation, faith or social status, as far removed from one's father or mother, brother or sister as possible. An heiress of one of the oldest American families elopes with a Chinese chauffeur, and a boy of an orthodox Jewish family falls in love with a blonde, gentile Norwegian girl. Another kind of avoidance, especially in sexual direction, is the search of an object outside one's own city or country. As a representative example I would like to point to the case of a Dutch young man who was impotent in The Hague which was his home town, but functioned sexually well in Amsterdam or Utrecht, cities only a short train ride away from The Hague. The rationalistic explanation of this divergence was, of course, that in The Hague many people knew him while the sexual secrecy could well be kept somewhere else. It was obvious that this was not the main reason for his sexual taboo. It was as if he had unconsciously identified his home town with his mother and sister, that means with sexually forbidden objects.

18. Morals and Humanity

Comparative anthropology and the history of religion, combined with psychoanalytic research, lead to the conclusion that the origin of morals is to be found in the tribal society of adult men. They forced the primal rules of conduct and the resulting principles upon the generation of adolescent youth of the tribe. Morals begin with don'ts and are first accompanied by threats and curses and severe punishment for the transgressors.

Humanity, it seems to me, originated in the relationship of mother and child. While the emergence of morals was necessitated by the vital requirements of the male society of the tribe, especially by the exigencies of maintaining the tribal group, humanity is founded on the more intimate feeling of the mother to whom the child is part of herself. The extension of this experience to the members of her family and finally to the group and all people results in what we call humanity. In the evolution of mankind morals are developed by men, humanity is born by women.

19. MEN, WOMEN AND NATURE

Any observer will find that women in general have a greater ability to identify with inorganic objects than do men. Psychologists and sociologists have pointed out that this gift of easy identification is the result of different emotional and educational factors. It seems to me that an important element has perhaps been neglected in research of this kind. It might help to explain this phenomenon; namely that woman's view of the world is unconsciously or preconsciously still preanimistic. We call preanimistic a phase of evolution in which nature is considered personalized and animated. A table, a chair, a cloud, a rock, all appear in this concept as having wills and souls of their own. They are alive and share the vicissitudes of living beings. We are not astonished when we hear a woman in a garden say, "Look at the poor tulips! They look miserable and they will certainly die!" Women look at flowers and plants as though they were children, and taking care of them is a continuation of child care. It is more astonishing to us men that women consider also pieces of furniture or pieces of cloth as living things. This means that women can live at the same time in this our age of science and technological progress, and in an early phase of the stone age. Women are, in their thinking and their concept of the world, nearer to nature than men. Only the poets seem to reach that intimacy with nature attained by women who have not removed themselves so far from their mother, the Earth. The animistic view is to be found again in the fairy tale in which also inorganic objects speak.

20. Love and Creation

It seems to me that the analogy between the emotional process of love and creativity, occasionally mentioned in psychological literature, has not been pursued thoroughly enough. For both, the totalitarian demand on the ego is characteristic. There is the miracle of the disappearance of the self and of selfishness, yes even of the frontiers between the self and the other creatures. In love and creation there is the same elation, coupled with humbleness, of a felicity which brings up the happiness of being open to the newness of people and things. Separateness of the individual has disappeared and the person feels united with the world around him and has a new respect for other existences. Love and creativity perform the miracle of this transformation without regard to the objective value of their objects: an artist will feel elated and happy whether his work is good, bad, or mediocre. A man will fall in love with an ugly woman as easily as with a very beautiful one. Love and creation are both works of art providing their objects with a unique excellence. All the world loves a lover, but the greater miracle is that a lover loves all the world in the overflow of his feelings of a bliss that has its only source in himself. Romeo feels that all creatures around him are as happy as he:

> ... heaven is here;
> Where Juliet lives; and every cat and dog
> And little mouse, every unworthy thing,
> Live here in heaven and may look at her.
> (Act III. Scene III.)

21. DIFFERENT VALUES

You call yourself a man and you are unable to conquer a place for yourself in the world of men? You call yourself a woman and you are unable to conquer the heart of a man and hold him for some time?

A psychoanalyst is not a moralist and the problems of ethics are remote from the area of his clinical interests. Yet after several decades of analytic practice he cannot avoid arriving at certain general evaluations for men and women. That means seeing them also from the point of view of their cultural value or their value for society. I arrived at such a scale, which is, of course, purely subjective. It is perhaps worth some thoughts or reflections although it is not binding for others. In my view or as I see it, a man should in the ideal case fulfill four requirements: he should be a good husband, a good father, a good provider and he should accomplish something remarkable in his field. This is, I repeat, the ideal case. He has, it seems to me, at least to fulfill two of those four demands to justify the name of a socially valuable person. It does not matter which two of the four are considered. A woman should, in the ideal case, fulfill three requirements: she should be a good wife, a good mother and a good mistress. It is, however, enough to fulfill two of these three demands in order to be considered a valuable and useful member of society.

PART TWELVE

Reflections on Sayings of Freud

(The following paragraphs do not belong, strictly speaking, in the area of the subject discussed in this book. But here are recounted some anecdotes of Freud's, and some of his remarks are quoted that seem to me well worth preserving and transmitting to the younger generation.)

I sometimes now think how well-organized and smooth the training of young psychoanalysts has become in contrast with the difficult times we had in the years of learning our profession. Now a young analyst who has gone through his own training-analysis and has attended all prescribed classes and seminars will be supervised in treating his own cases by an older, experienced psychoanalyst. Those supervision sessions are regular and are used to discuss the psychological and technical problems of the cases. (We had in Vienna usually five or six sessions weekly with our patients, and we spoke jokingly of a "Sunday crust" that formed itself over the weekend and which we had to scrape away on Monday.)

When we were faced with the many difficulties and puzzled by various contradictions in psychoanalytic practice, we went to Berggasse 19 and we asked Freud's advice. He always listened patiently and was generous in giving us his views. I am now in a situation of a psychoanalytic supervisor or control-analyst myself, and I sometimes remember those informal conversations I had in my early years with my teacher.

From time to time, various incidents revivify my memory, and some characteristic remarks of Freud come to mind. A severely masochistic patient showed during a certain phase of the psychoanalytic treatment a very defiant and rebellious attitude towards me, although previously he had been mostly submissive and passive. I remembered a similar case I had treated more than thirty years ago and which I discussed with Freud. During this conversation I expressed my astonishment about the contrast of the rebellious and aggressive attitude of that patient with his previous masochistic behavior. Freud said that the change was only superficial and could be explained by the fact that the unconscious masochistic desires of the patient had found no satisfaction in his psychoanalytic sessions and that his recent provocative behavior indicated that they had become more urgent and demanded gratification. "It is," Freud said, "as if the patient raises his nude behind into the air and wishes you would hit him there."

In fact Freud, who soon recognized a masochist trend in my own personality had said to me at the end of a psychoanalytic session, "You do not admit your faults, but boast of them."

During the political crisis in Austria the clerical party and the Communists and left-wing socialists came into a long and dramatic conflict. The first party was generally called "black" in Vienna, while the socialists were characterized as "the reds." Freud once expressed his bewilderment about this name-giving, adding that in his opinion people should be "flesh-colored."

Once Dr. Oscar Pfister, the Zürich pastor who applied psychoanalytic methods in ministry, and I waited together in

Freud's office for our teacher who had an appointment with us. Freud had a German professor of psychiatry as visitor and could not get rid of the man, whose conversation bored him. Freud came into the waiting-room for a minute, apologized to us for the lateness and turning to Dr. Pfister, asked, "Tell me, does Christianity still forbid killing people even in thoughts?"

Freud considered America as matriarchy. He sometimes quoted the old sentence that the best woman is the one who is not talked about.

Here is an instance of the comparisons he used to illustrate the emotional dynamics of cases. A patient of mine showed a strange and paradoxical behavior-pattern in his professional life: he always came very close to reaching a great success, but failed by some diverting or insignificant pleasure he allowed himself when he was just within reach of his aims. He failed, so to speak, in sight of his goal. The masochistic and self-sabotaging character of his behavior was obvious. Freud, with whom I discussed the case said, "He acts like a man who returns from a long journey home in a cold winter night. He already sees the lighted windows of his home and he needs only a little effort to arrive at home. But he falls in to the next pub on the road."

Freud repeatedly emphasized that the coming late of the patient to his analytic sessions has the conscious significance of resistance, of a reluctance to come at all. He refused to acknowledge the various reasons patients brought forth for their delay and interpreted them as rationalizations. He said, "In these cases—a few exceptions admitted—a psychoanalyst should adopt the point of view of a woman. When the man says he is too late on a date because there was a long business meeting or an important telephone call, she is seemingly unreasonable and says, 'Yes, but last year when you loved me more you were always on time.' "

Freud insisted that the patient should tell his analyst the names of the persons who are important in his life (wife, children, brothers and sisters). Freud said that we unconsciously connect certain ideas with names. When in psychoanalysis the patient speaks of his wife, his older brother and younger sister or his friend without mentioning their names, it is as if you are in a play whose characters are nameless and are qualified only as father, mother, wife, friend and so on. Names of relatives of our patients are not only mnemotechnically important to us. The very fact that the patient in speaking of them avoids to call them by their names is psychologically significant.

Freud once said to us that telling children the facts of life almost always occurs too late. The children have already formed infantile sexual theories which are sometimes a grotesque combination of fact and fiction. Sexual enlightenment given to children, said Freud, resembles thus the view an uneducated woman expressed at the time about a play by Arthur Schnitzler performed in the Vienna Burgtheater. Mrs. Pollak, of the nouveau riche, was asked during the intermission how she liked the play. She said, "The play is very nice, but it does not fit for an opening night."

At one of those Wednesday evenings when Freud in his old age saw a small circle of his students at his home, he discussed the emotional reaction brought about by the process of repression. He chose an analogous example from the life of children. "You all know," he said, "that many children violently refuse to eat spinach. It is easy to guess why spinach preconsciously reminds them of stool by its substance or color. We know that infants are not disgusted by their feces.

They play with them and eat them. Their abhorrence of feces is a result of early education, sometimes of a too abrupt or too early toilet training. That what these children once liked very much becomes by this process the subject of sickening dislike."

I once discussed with Freud the case of a neurotic patient whose sadistic trends were obvious, but had remained repressed. Reacting to my astonishment that the patient could not conquer those unconscious tendencies, Freud said, "You can't kill a person who is not present."

Freud speaking to me about the necessity of changing the classical psychoanalytic technique in certain neurotic cases said, "Under special circumstances you have to mix the pure gold of psychoanalysis with baser metals."

A critical sentence Freud said to me at the end of a psychoanalytic session has often reoccurred to me in later years. During that phase of my life my wife had serious heart troubles and was in a sanatorium. Leaving her after my daily visit there I was often taken by sudden spells of violent dizziness. In analytical sessions Freud arrived at the conclusion that those attacks were reactions to repressed death-wishes against my wife and unconsciously represented so to speak my dying as self-punishment for those evil wishes. At the time of that after-analysis with Freud I had been an analyst myself for many years, but had not understood that I was the stage-manager behind the wings who produced those attacks as punishment for my thought crime. At the end of the session Freud said, "I would have thought you stronger" ("*Ich hätte Sie für stärker gehalten*"), alluding to the delicacy of my conscience. His sentence, often remembered in the following years, made me blush in mortification.

PART THIRTEEN

Psychological Notes

1. Problems of Psychoanalytic Technique

The psychoanalyst can in a great number of neurotic cases do no more than bring his patient far enough to enable him to make a decision after he has regained his energy and acquired a clear insight into the nature of his fundamental conflicts. The situation thus evolving resembles one to be found in certain stories of O. Henry in which the leading character finds himself on a crossroad and in which his destiny depends on his choice of the road he will follow.

When the analytic treatment has reached this critical point, the patient has not only an intellectual understanding of his difficulties, but is often able to master them emotionally. At this point all depends on the moral courage he develops in the crisis. The situation reminds me of another in which an athlete recognized that his opponent tried to evade a decisive match with him using different pretexts. The athlete said about the other: "When I have him once in the ring, he can run away, but he can't hide any longer from me." The critical point is reached when the patient is ready to face his inner adversary. He has to step into the arena: he might then run away from his antagonist but he cannot hide any longer from him.

The psychoanalytic technique in the treatment of social

or psychic masochism seems at first to aggravate the emotional state of the patient, but the burden that is apparently added to his load operates in reality as a relief. First of all the analyst will not fail to tell the patient that the work looming before him will be difficult and demands great sacrifices. The analyst cannot promise victory except when the patient becomes willing to accept this premise. The psychotherapist has thus "nothing to offer but blood, toil, tears, and sweat" as Winston Churchill told us in his speech at the House of Commons in May 1940.

Yet the patient holds a prospect of redemption after the great sacrifice is suffered. There is another feature in the treatment of social masochism which differs from the technique applied in the psychoanalysis of neurotics: the psychoanalyst will make the patient face the unconscious guilt for which he atones in his self-inflicted suffering. Also this unrestricted and blunt formulation of the thought-crime for which the patient punishes himself will often be experienced as an addition to his misery, but will pave the way to emotional relief. Almost everyone has listened to Edgar Bergen with his dummy Charley McCarthy. Once Mr. Bergen, in a despondent mood, sighingly says, "I am my own worst enemy." McCarthy says, "Not when I'm around." In a similar way the analyst apparently takes over the role of the accuser. But this amounts only to a new distribution—the externalization of the self-accusation means a considerable emotional relief. The conflict that divided the self is now brought not only into the open, but outside the self and a better chance to conquer it is thus advanced. To attempt another comparison: before the last war America's political life was characterized by a furious battle of contending parties. Then came the Japanese attack. Overnight our country was united in the fight against the enemy from outside. All inner conflict had vanished in the common battle.

Only after the patient has faced the unconscious guilt-feeling in which his self-sabotage and self-punishment originate can the inner discussion about the character of the inner verdict at which the patient arrived be contested. An inner court has sentenced him to failure and isolation and so on. The psychoanalyst supports then the efforts of the patient to secure a revision of the sentence.

It is to continue the comparison, as if now the moment has come to appeal to a higher court and to have the case heard again before the inner judge. It will be argued that the sentence imposed was much too severe and perhaps even brutally injust. It is as if a man who stole a loaf of bread were sentenced to several years of solitary confinement combined with forced labor. There is a fair possibility that the court appealed to will reexamine and reverse the decisions of the unconscious court which had condemned the culprit.

2. The Mystery of Feminine Sexuality

The French and the Dutch psychoanalysts will have a convention in Holland early in September of this year (1960), and I have been invited to take part in the discussion of a paper on feminine sexuality. Dr. A. I. Westerman Holstijn, the Amsterdam psychiatrist, has sent me the script of the lecture he will give and asked me to comment on it. While I am studying his interesting paper, entitled "*Les organes genitaux fémins, l'orgasme et la frigidité*," many thoughts interfere with a cool and objective evaluation of the scientific contribution to psychology. There are memories of Holland, of the quiet and beautiful country in which I lived for a few years after I escaped the Nazis, pictures of The Hague, of Rotterdam and Amsterdam. And while I am attentively reading the survey of the literature on feminine sexuality, the impression occurs and reoccurs how little we still know about it. Women are and remain the mysterious sex and the area of their sexual sensations and emotions is not the least of their mysteries.

So many questions, simple and complex, are still unanswered or are given contradictory answers. There is the problem of feminine frigidity. Not even the sexologists and psychoanalysts seem to be able to agree about the definition of this term. While a part of them speak of frigidity as a case where the woman remains "cold" in sexual contact, others conceive of frigidity as absence of orgasm, even when the woman is sexually very excited. Putting aside the complex problem of frigidity and focusing on the question of feminine sexual experience, we encounter an unexpected difficulty, namely the almost incredible diversity in the descriptions women present about their sensations. Observations made by gynecologists and psychiatrists show that what appears to one woman as typical sexual experience, is for another of no significance and that even the localization of sexual experiences varies from one woman to the next. In psychoanalytic literature a sharp differentiation is made between clitoris orgasm and vaginal orgasm. Edmund Bergler states that women have two sexual organs, the clitoris and the vagina and considers the different theories about the feminine orgasm as results of this fact. The trouble is only that this is not a fact, but a fiction. There are other parts sensitive in women, for instance the vulva and the lips, and the feminine orgasm does not take place in a single organ, but in the whole organism. While the clitoris and the vagina have, so to speak, the leading roles, there are other actors on the stage. The clitoris and the vaginal sensations are decidedly different, but it is very possible that the place where the sexual excitement begins is not identical with the one where it is unleashed. We know that many women— some gynecologists assert even three quarters of all women— never experienced a vaginal orgasm. G. L. Kelly made the famous statement, "There are no frigid women, there are only unexperienced men." It is incontestable that many men approach their partner in such a stupid or gauche way that a normal woman has great difficulty in reaching sexual enjoyment. Yet that sentence certainly is an overstatement and can be compared to Gustav Mahler's assertion that there are no bad orchestras, only bad conductors.

Not to mention the many cases of neurotic and psychotic women, there are a great number of women who, as Marie Bonaparte points out, need a certain time to adapt themselves to the sexual function and afterwards reach the sexual climax. It is even questionable that the orgasm is as important for the woman as for the man. It is certainly a mistake to declare that most women who do not reach an orgasm are emotionally sick. Many of those "anorgastic" women feel that they are satisfied in sexual intercourse and become neurotic only when the husband is angry with them or tries to help them by masturbatory practices. Recent researches, including Westerman Holstijn in his paper mentioned above, assert that one has to differentiate between sexual satisfaction and paroxysm whereby only the latter, mostly of a very short duration, can be called orgasm in its narrow sense. Yes, there are women who know both forms and are able to describe their differences. If this concept is correct and if one would accept a wider terminology including also that emotional satisfaction into the notion of orgasm, then woman has two forms of orgasm, while man knows only one. Many women assert that the second form of voluptuous satisfaction is more diffuse, of much longer duration and more extensive than the orgastic paroxysm.

There are many other crucial questions concerning the feminine sexual satisfaction. Some of them do not belong to the area of psychology and psychoanalysis, but can be approached only by applying biological methods. Quite a few of these problems have to wait for their solution until new biological findings clarify the differences between masculine and feminine sexuality.

In a recent French movie a woman says to a man who is in an emotional conflict, *"L'amour est si simple."* Contrary to conventional views love is not a complicated problem for woman. It vexes man more. But feminine sexuality is still a mystery not only to man who will perhaps never understand it, but to woman herself.

The coming meeting in Holland reminds me that I am constitutionally unable to give a formal lecture, to put a manuscript at a desk and read it. At best I can deliver a chat, something similar to what the French call *"une causerie."* I remember the first lecture I gave before the Vienna Psychoanalytic Society. On the way home Freud praised the lecture, but was critical about my needing to read from the manuscript. I remember that he said a speaker should speak freely as if the content and the forms of his lecture were the product of his present trains of thoughts. Only in this way does the speaker give his listeners an opportunity to "think with him." If, said Freud, a lecturer reads from a prepared manuscript he is comparable to a man who invited some people for an auto ride, but drives alone and lets the others run after the car. Since this admonition I have become unable to give a formal lecture.

I am still shy during the first minute or so, but help myself by making a joke or telling an anecdote which gets me over the initial embarrassment. Here is an instance of such an introduction to a lecture delivered after the chairman had presented me to the audience in some eulogistic sentences. "Ladies and gentlemen: When you are invited to a cocktail party or some other social gathering and the hostess introduced you adding 'You know, the psychoanalyst,' or similarly, you have occasion to observe some typical reactions of the guests to you. Some of them avoid you because you are a 'headshrinker,' some try to pump you and ask you what a certain dream means and some tell you jokes about psychoanalysis. At a party the other day a man sat down beside me and said, 'I just have to tell you a funny story. An actor comes to a psychoanalyst to consult him and tells him all his complaints: "I don't have a good articulation, I don't know what to do with the arms and legs when I am on the stage, I forget my lines, I have terrible stage fright" and he goes on and on. The psychoanalyst patiently listens to the patient and finally says: "Since you have so many difficulties in acting, wouldn't it be advisable to change your profession?" The patient replies, "You see, that's difficult. I am a star on Broadway.'"

"I am in a situation similar to the patient in the story. Your chairman introduced me as a famous psychoanalyst and I am painfully aware of my shortcomings and defects. I cannot, for instance, give a formal lecture."

3. FRAGMENT OF A CONVERSATION
BETWEEN TWO PSYCHOLOGISTS

"You speak of a special psychological perceptiveness of women, compared with men," said George, who teaches experimental psychology in a Midwestern University. "Let me confess that I have not observed such a characteristic trait in the female students in my classes."

"You mean in controlled experimental work?" I asked. "Well, I am not competent to form an opinion there, but what I meant was really in everyday life."

"Can you give me an instance?"

"Here is one," I said. "A patient of mine—let's call her Mrs. Brown—told me in her psychoanalytic session that she and her husband visited first one family and later on another couple on Sunday evening. She said that at the first visit she had quite a good time, was interested in the people and took an active part in the conversation, but on the way to the second visit she already had become depressed and when she was with the second couple she felt somber and said very little although her husband, the other man and the woman had an interesting conversation."

"Perhaps she did not like the people whom she visited later on," said George.

"No, on the contrary, she liked the man and the woman was an old friend of hers. The difference in her mood had other reasons. Mrs. Brown is married to an engineer who is fifteen years older than she and they lived quite happily together until two years ago. Then her husband became involved in an affair with a typist in his office, an affair which threatened to be rather serious and which led to several violent scenes between husband and wife. He still sees that girl daily, takes her out, and no doubt sleeps with her. Now, my patient tries her best to put up a good front and to hide her depression when she is with people, but she does not always succeed."

George said, "Of course not. She did not at the second visit."

"It's not as simple as that. She told me herself why she could cover up her bad mood at the first visit and not at the second. The people she and her husband saw first don't know anything of that affair, but the couple they visited afterwards know all about it, are familiar with all its details." ·

"And that made so much difference?" asked George.

"Of course. I can't blame you because I myself did not focus on that point and thought Mrs. Brown had to exert determined self-control at the first visit and could release it with the couple who were friends. But there you see how obtuse we psychologists are in psychological things. When she reminded me that the second couple knew about her husband's affair I understood, of course. . . ."

"You understood what, Theodor?"

"The change of her mood."

"It's still not clear to me."

"It's simple enough. Don't you see what a difference it makes to a woman when she is with people who know that her husband prefers another and younger girl to her? Don't you understand that she feels defeated? That couple had known Mr. and Mrs. Brown and had thought they were happily married and now they realize that the wife is miserable because her husband is in bondage to an inferior, promiscuous hussy."

"Well," said George thoughtfully, "you have a point there."

"Just the point I want to drive home. Do you believe a woman, any woman to whom you tell this story, would have missed the signals? Would not any woman have caught them and immediately have understood what difference it must have made for Mrs. Brown that the second couple knew and felt sorry for her? Such things are, of course, not contained in the textbooks of psychology or psychoanalysis. We men have to be told, but every woman is perceptive enough so that you need not explain them. Isn't there a play by James Barrie, *What Every Woman Knows?*"

Postlude in ¾ Time

When Fred came to see me the calendar already denoted 1960 and we were in the middle of winter. When I offered him a cigarette, he told me that he had stopped smoking. I poured coffee into his cup and he said, "Very light, please— on advice of my physician!" We chatted.

"How far are you along with your novel?" I asked.

"Some parts are still in their first draft, and some in their seventh and eighth. You know how it is with writing."

"Where is the difficulty?" I inquired.

"Difficulties, you mean. There is, first of all, the problem of style. The question is not what to say but how to say it. The internal monologue, going on in the girl and in the young man, has to be informal and chatty—almost clipped. The narrative will be smooth, subtle and sophisticated. It's not easy to make it sound this way. Anatole France, you know, recommended to a young writer, '*Caressez votre phrase!*'"

"You writers!" I said, full of envy, "everything is—or becomes—play for you. You are flirting, even with language.

When we wish to write a scientific paper it is hard work and drudgery. We plane away like a carpenter until we are exhausted."

"We do some of that too sometimes," said Fred. Then suddenly he asked, "Isn't the monument of Raimund in front of the Deutsche Volkstheater?"

I was so startled that I almost spilled my coffee. I too had thought of Ferdinand Raimund just then. I had not thought of the white statue of the writer sitting in front of the theater —I had passed it quite a few times the summer before in Vienna—I had rather thought of the "Song of the Plane" sung in Raimund's folkplay *The Spendthrift*, whose first performance took place in 1880 and which is still sometimes played in Viennese theaters. The comparison of toilsome writing with planing must have awakened in both of us the memory of that unforgettable Viennese folksong which we had both heard as boys. For a fleeting moment the figure of the tragic poet Raimund had emerged in my memory. Along with it had appeared the expressive face of the actor, Alexander Girardi, whom I had seen performing the part of the leading character in Raimund's fairy play, and who had sung the Song of the Plane in his inimitable manner. The plot of that folkplay remained at the fringes of my thoughts. Only the figure of the carpenter Valentin, who sings the "Hobellied" in broad Viennese dialect plastically stepped on the stage of my memory. The initial words of that song, *"Da streiten sich die Leut' herum,"* along with its tune in ¾ time, resounded in me.

"Wait a minute, Fred," I said, and went over to the drawer in which I had put several souvenirs brought back from Vienna. Among them were quite a few records, including the

"Song of the Plane," sung by Leo Slezak. I found this record and put it on. We listened to the old song:

> "There are those people fighting still
> For things that come and go
> They call each other names at will
> At the end they nothing know
>
> Here proudly rides too rich a man
> The poorest there must hike
> But fortune moves and with its plane
> Planes rich and poor alike
>
> The youth so happy and so bold
> Are always after fun
> But let them get a little old
> Not so fast will they run."

At this point Fred interrupted the carpenter's wise and folksy song. I lifted the needle. "Wouldn't it be funny," he said, "if my novel and your essay were our last books before we die? Both are unsubstantial and light as a soufflé. . . . Don't you think it is rather an undignified leave-taking of two serious writers?"

"Well," I said, "when the chips, or rather the shavings are down, it's not important any longer. I read the other day what a British statesman—was it not Charles Fox?—said on his deathbed, 'It don't signify.' But listen!"

I put the needle back. While we listened we were both very aware that the lines related to us old fellows:

> When death—forgive the word!—appears
> And whispers, "Brother come!"
> I wish I had still many years
> And play both deaf and dumb.

But says he, "My friend Valentine,
Don't make a fuss, don't cry!
I'll put my plane into the shrine
And bid the world 'Good bye.'"

Fred was still gloomy.

"Cheer up!" I said, "a novelist will perhaps write best about woman in his seventies."

"But who the hell wants to write about women when he is in his seventies?"

I looked at him. He had to laugh at his own grimness.